T0303381

TALES FROM THE
PURDUE BOILERMAKERS
LOCKER ROOM

A COLLECTION OF THE GREATEST
BOILERMAKER STORIES EVER TOLD

DOUG GRIFFITHS,
ALAN KARPICK,
AND TOM SCHOTT

SPORTS
PUBLISHING

Copyright © 2003 by Doug Griffiths, Alan Karpick, and Tom Schott
First Skyhorse Publishing edition 2015

Sports Publishing books may be purchased in bulk at special discounts for sales promotion, corporate gifts, fund-raising, or educational purposes. Special editions can also be created to specifications. For details, contact the Special Sales Department, Sports Publishing, 307 West 36th Street, 11th Floor, New York, NY 10018 or sportspubbooks@skyhorsepublishing.com.

Sports Publishing® is a registered trademark of Skyhorse Publishing, Inc.®, a Delaware corporation.

Visit our website at www.sportspubbooks.com.

10 9 8 7 6 5 4 3

Library of Congress Cataloging-in-Publication Data is available on file.

Series jacket design by Tom Lau
Jacket photograph by AP Images

Print ISBN: 978-1-61321-777-1

Printed in China

Dedication

To my wife, Kim, and our precious daughter, Abbie, for all your love and support during this endeavor. You are and always will be my number one fans and make my life so fulfilling. And to my mother, Alice Anne, and grandfather (aka Gammy John). Without your unconditional love and tremendous support while I was growing up, I would never be where I am today. And to the Boilermaker coaches, players and administrators who have allowed me to honestly say I have a job that I love 365 days a year.

—D.G.

To Amy, Reid and Hayley for your love and support. And to my father, Ed Karpick, and the many coaches and players for sharing the great stories of Purdue sports with me.

—A.K.

To Jane, August and Sam—my home team. And to the coaches and student athletes I have worked with at Purdue over the last 13 years—it truly has been a labor of love.

—T.S.

Contents

Acknowledgments

The authors would like to thank the following individuals for taking time to share their "tales" over the years: Dave Alexander, Otis Armstrong, Roger Blalock, Drew Brees, Morgan Burke, Bart Burrell, Leon Burtnett, Larry Burton, Dave Butz, Brian Cardinal, Nancy Cross, Len Dawson, Bob DeMoss, Lin Dunn, George Faerber, Jerry Jackson, Gene Keady, Frank Kendrick, Leroy Keyes, Bob King, John Konsek, Cindy Lamping, Troy Lewis, Shannon Lindsey, Clyde Lyle, Cuonzo Martin, Denny Miller, Rick Mount, Dave Rankin, Steve Reid, Glenn Robinson, Henry Rosenthal, Pete Quinn, Stephen Scheffler, Brock Spack, Hank Stram, Darryl Stingley, Joe Tiller, Bruce Weber, John Wooden, Rod Woodson and Jim Young.

We also would like to thank Mike Pearson and Gabe Rosen of Sports Publishing L.L.C. for helping make this book a reality.

Photos courtesy of Tom Campbell, Purdue University Photo and Digital, and Purdue University Sports Information archives.

Introduction

Tales from the Purdue Boilermakers Locker Room is a compilation of some of the great stories that we have experienced during our combined 80 years of watching, covering and administrating Purdue University athletics. Many have been told to us from one person's perspective and may innocently fall short of the hard facts of a particular event, but therein lies the charm of this book.

While not intended to be a complete history of Boilermaker sports, Tales from the Purdue Boilermakers Locker Room gives you a flavor of many of the great names, events and accomplishments of over 115 years of intercollegiate competition. Whether they are funny, poignant or tragic, Tales from the Purdue Boilermakers Locker Room celebrates the rich tradition that is Purdue athletics.

Doug Griffiths
Alan Karpick
Tom Schott

Foreword by Joe Tiller

A s the head football coach at Purdue University, I
am, obviously, a Purdue fan. I'm also a history
buff. That combination best sums up *Tales from the Purdue
Boilermakers Locker Room.*

Doug Griffiths, Alan Karpick and Tom Schott have done
a wonderful job of retelling more than 200 stories about
Purdue athletics over the past 100-plus years. I know these
guys are good, but you will be convinced that they in fact
were around when David Ross and George Ade donated the
land for Ross-Ade Stadium in 1924. They have conducted
numerous interviews and done extensive research.

The word "tales" is most appropriate for the title,
because the stories are just that, written in an easy-to-read,
conversational style. When you read them, you will feel like
you and a buddy are sitting in the family room, talking over
a bowl of chips and an ice-cold drink.

During my first stint at Purdue as an assistant coach
in the 1980s, I quickly discovered that Purdue fans love to
reminisce about Boilermaker lore, more so than any other
place I had been. Nearly 20 years later, I can honestly say
nothing has changed. If you are one of those people—and
I'm sure you are—you definitely will enjoy *Tales from the
Purdue Boilermakers Locker Room.*

Boiler Up!

Joe Tiller
August 2003

CHAPTER 1

Pre-1950s

Why Boilermakers?

One of the most frequently asked questions of Purdue fans is about the origin of the school's unique nickname, "Boilermakers." Following is the official explanation as presented in the athletic department's publicity materials:

The year was 1891, and a little-known school that prided itself on educating men and women for productive, utilitarian careers was just beginning to experience success in football. DePauw, Wabash and Butler were the football powers of Indiana in those days. Purdue was late to the game, fielding its first team in 1887 and losing its only game to Butler 48-6.

By 1891, Purdue had hired two coaches from eastern power Princeton and was on the verge of an era of total domination of opponents. In the 1891 season opener, Purdue traveled to Wabash College in nearby Crawfordsville. Besides coming away with a 44-0 victory, the Purdue "eleven," as football teams were known back then, headed back to West Lafayette with a new nickname.

In the 1890s, hometown newspapers were considerably more protective of college teams than they are today. After the 44-0 drubbing, one Crawfordsville newspaper lashed out at the

"Herculean wearers of the black and old gold." Beneath the headline "Slaughter of Innocents," the paper told of the injustice visited upon the "light though plucky" Wabash squad.

"Wabash Snowed Completely Under by the Burly Boiler Makers from Purdue" proclaimed another headline on the same story in the *Daily Argus-News*.

By the next week, the Lafayette papers were returning the taunts: "As everyone knows, Purdue went down to Wabash last Saturday and defeated their eleven. The Crawfordsville papers have not yet gotten over it. The only recourse they have is to claim that we beat their 'scientific' men by brute force. Our players are characterized as 'coal heavers,' 'boiler makers' and 'stevedores,'" wrote a reporter for the *Lafayette Sunday Times* of November 1, 1891.

The nickname stemmed from the nature of a Purdue education. As a land-grant institution, the college, since its founding in 1869, had schooled the sons and daughters of the working class for work that was considered beneath the highborn who attended liberal arts colleges such as Wabash.

That same fall of 1891, Purdue had acquired a working railroad engine to mount in a newly established locomotive laboratory. It was one more step in the development of Purdue as one of the world's leaders in engineering teaching and research. For athletic adversaries and their boosters, this specialty in engineering education—and the other concentration at the founding of the institution, agriculture—served as fodder for name-calling.

Over the years, Purdue teams had been called grangers, pumpkin-shuckers, railsplitters, cornfield sailors, blacksmiths, foundry hands and, finally, boilermakers. That last one stuck.

"A" for Ames

Knowlton Ames was the fourth football coach in Purdue history, yet he is credited with being the one who put the Boilermakers on the map.

Purdue lost the only game it played in its debut season of 1887, did not field a team in 1888 and won five of nine contests in 1889 and 1890. Then Ames came to West Lafayette from Chicago, along with his comrade, Ben Donnelly. "What a piece of luck it was when those two lads consented to come down and take charge of our disorganized and beaten outfit and hammer it into a team!" wrote Purdue alum and noted playwright George Ade in the November 16, 1929, issue of *Liberty Weekly*.

Both Ames, who was nicknamed "Snake," and Donnelly, who answered to "Sport," had been prominent players at Princeton, the premier team of the East. One of their teammates was the legendary Edgar Allen Poe. At Purdue, Ames coached the backs and developed the game plans, while Donnelly worked with the line. Over the next two seasons, the Boilermakers were never beaten, going 12-0.

But Purdue didn't just win, it dominated, completely shutting out all four 1891 opponents 192-0 and outscoring its eight 1892 foes 320-24. Along the way, the Boilermakers won the first two of four consecutive Indiana Intercollegiate Athletic Association championships.

In a 1929 letter to Ade, Ames remarked, "The Purdue teams for the two years when Donnelly and I were coaching were about the best in the country and had about as good material in them as I ever saw, and you cannot speak too highly of all the boys."

Ames, a member of the College Football Hall of Fame, and Donnelly stayed at Purdue for only two years, but they left an indelible mark that has been felt for more than a century.

Smart Decision

J ames Henry Smart, who served as Purdue president from 1883 to 1900, is regarded as the man who established the conference known now as the Big Ten. Smart's desire to form such a conference to oversee athletic competition stemmed mostly from the infiltration of professional teams competing against college students during the early 1890s.

Smart wanted to "preserve college athletics from the demoralization of professionalism," and the Purdue faculty passed an order on January 1, 1895, prohibiting its teams from playing any professional or semiprofessional teams.

Purdue, which had won four consecutive championships as a member of the Indiana Intercollegiate Athletic Association, took issue with Butler playing a professional team called Light Artillery on Thanksgiving Day 1894—the same day Purdue defeated DePauw 28-0 in Indianapolis to win the IIAA crown.

Against Smart's wishes, Butler played Light Artillery, and Smart pushed on with the formation of the Western Conference. On January 11, 1895, Smart called a meeting of seven Midwestern schools and didn't invite Butler, setting the table for the formation of the new league.

Smart must have had a quick change of heart about playing professional teams like Light Artillery. Purdue had beaten Light Artillery 6-4 earlier in that season. The Boilermakers never met Butler again in Smart's lifetime. The two teams next met on the gridiron in 1902, two years after Smart's death.

Had Butler not been defiant, it is likely it would have been asked to join the Western Conference. Had that happened, Indiana University, which was not one of the original seven schools to join, might have been passed over to join the new league.

Why the Boilermakers Wear Black

I t was Halloween 1903, and the Boilermaker football team was on its way to face archrival Indiana. A long line of people in the Boilermaker travel party made its way into the train station in Indianapolis. The last train, which carried the Purdue football team, waited, as the train ahead of it was about to come to a stop.

Then, seemingly out of nowhere, an engine steamrolled through an open switch and hit a car full of Purdue players broadside. In the carnage, 16 Boilermakers were killed and a couple dozen more injured. The team essentially was wiped out of existence.

Through the rubble came one great story of survival. With numerous broken bones and several subsequent surgeries, "Skillet" Leslie wasn't supposed to survive. Like the Purdue football program, Leslie lived for a greater day, so much so that he became Governor Harry Leslie of Indiana from 1929 to 1933 before his death at age 59 in 1937.

The I-vies Have It

N ine of the 33 head football coaches in Purdue history graduated from Ivy League schools. Five of the first six were Princeton alums: Albert Berg (1887), C.L. Hare (1890), Knowlton Ames (1891-92), D.M. Balliet (1893-95 and 1901) and S.M. Hammond (1896). The other four Ivy Leaguers were G.A. Reisner (1889), Oliver F. Cutts (1903-04) and M.E. Witham (1906) from Harvard and L.C. Turner (1907) from Dartmouth.

Three Purdue alums subsequently coached at their alma mater: Alpha P. Jamison (1898-1900), Cecil Isbell (1944-46) and Bob DeMoss (1970-72),

Bachelors Build Ross-Ade

George Ade, a humorist, and David Ross, an engineer who made steering components for early automobiles, were wealthy bachelors. They also were benefactors to Purdue University, purchasing 65 acres of land just north of campus and establishing the Ross-Ade Foundation. They agreed to someday put a stadium on the land. The pair knew that the glacial formation had left a hole on the property they owned that would make for a perfect stadium bowl.

Ross, a quiet fellow, was growing impatient in the early 1920s. He called up Ade and reportedly convinced him that the pair was not getting any younger. Ross thought that if the stadium was going to be built in their lifetimes, they better get moving.

Ross and Ade participated in a fundraising campaign where the duo agreed to match contributions by alumni purchasing "lifetime" seats. A couple of years later, Ross-Ade Stadium was built. It was dedicated in fine fashion as Purdue defeated Indiana 26-7 in the first game in its history on November 22, 1924.

Until We Meet Again

Little did Guy "Red" Mackey and Fred Hovde know what the future held when Purdue and Minnesota met on the football field on October 13, 1928.

The Golden Gophers won 15-0, as Hovde, their quarterback, ran for a touchdown and passed to set up the other on a run by the legendary Bronko Nagurski. Mackey, meanwhile, was a senior end for the Boilermakers.

Their paths would cross again years later at Purdue. Mackey served as athletics director from 1942 to 1971, while Hovde was president from 1946 to 1971. The two formed a fast friendship that included routine dates on the golf course.

Both Hovde and Mackey presided over some of the most

glorious days in Purdue history. During Hovde's reign, enrollment increased from 5,628 to 25,582, and the school emerged as a top research university. Mackey occupied the AD's office when the Boilermakers captured the 1961 NCAA men's golf championship, won the 1967 Rose Bowl and advanced to the 1969 NCAA Tournament's Final Four.

Campus landmarks Mackey Arena (1972) and Hovde Hall (1975) are named in honor of the two men.

Making Coin on the Train

B efore athletic scholarships came into being in the 1950s, college athletes had to earn money any way they could to pay for tuition and room and board. Some students proved to be more industrious than others. All-American basketball players Stretch Murphy and John Wooden fell into that category.

During Murphy's senior year, he secured the "rights" to sell concessions on the train full of Purdue football fans headed from Lafayette for a game against the University of Chicago on October 26, 1929. The Boilermakers were at the midway point of their only undisputed Big Ten football title season in school history.

Wooden learned the trade so well from teammate and pal Murphy that after Murphy's graduation, he ran the concessions himself for two years. He was not one for drinking and carrying on, but he knew how to serve those who liked to imbibe a little.

"I learned one thing," Wooden would say years later, "the closer the train got to Chicago, the bigger the tips were."

During his coaching days that spanned 10 NCAA titles, Wooden learned how to manage some free spirits on his team like Bill Walton and Sidney Wicks. Apparently during his college days, Wooden knew a thing or two about working with free spirits, as well.

John Wooden

Westward Ho

Purdue fans are familiar with the University of Washington from the two schools' meeting in the 2001 Rose Bowl and the 2002 Sun Bowl. Though the Boilermakers and Huskies have met on the football field just 10 times—all since 1961—their ties date more than 70 years.

In 1929, the Boilermakers, coached by Jim Phelan, enjoyed their first undefeated, untied season of the 20th century at 8-0 and won the only outright Big Ten championship in school history. One of their stars was halfback Ralph "Pest" Welch, who was named one of the first two All-Americans ever at Purdue in 1929.

One year later, both Phelan and Welch were in Washington.

Phelan served as head coach of the Huskies from 1930 to 1941, while Welch was an assistant for all but one (1938) of those 12 seasons. When Phelan left Seattle for St. Mary's (Calif.), Welch succeeded him and piloted Washington for six years.

At Purdue, Phelan compiled a 35-22-5 record from 1922 to 1929. He ranks tied for fifth on the school's all-time wins list. After posting a 3-10-2 record during his first two seasons, he went 32-13-3 over his final six campaigns. At Washington, Phelan had a 65-37-8 record and led the Huskies to the 1937 Rose Bowl and the 1938 Pineapple Bowl.

Phelan later coached professionally with the New York Titans, New York Yankees, Baltimore Colts and Texas Rangers. He subsequently got involved in politics and served three terms as county commissioner for Sacramento County in California while becoming a personal friend of then-governor Ronald Reagan. Phelan was inducted into the College Football Hall of Fame in 1973. He died November 14, 1979, at the age of 81.

The Boilermakers' 1929 backfield was dubbed the "Four Riveters," in playing off the nickname "Boilermakers" and recalling the fabled "Four Horsemen" of Notre Dame from 1924. Along with Welch were quarterback John White, fullback Alex Yunevich and halfback Glen Harmeson.

Welch's six seasons in Washington, including an appearance in the 1944 Rose Bowl, were marked by the turmoil caused by World War II, with players coming and going as their war duties allowed. He managed a 27-20-3 record. Welch was inducted into the Purdue Intercollegiate Athletics Hall of Fame in 2003.

It Wasn't a Blast for Lambert

B oilermaker fans who have seen them both say there are some striking similarities between the sideline antics of legendary coaches Gene Keady and Ward "Piggy" Lambert. While much smaller in stature than Keady, Lambert had his moments of wildness on the sideline.

During the 1933-34 season, Purdue played all of its home games in Lafayette Jefferson High School. The Boilermakers had outgrown the small capacity of Memorial Gym on campus and needed the 5,000-plus seats across town. In one crazy game against Iowa, Lambert ran toward the scorers' table to dispute a call just before a foul was whistled. He arrived in time for the timer to fire the final gun, which subsequently gave Lambert a mild case of tetanus from the gunpowder blast. Iowa won the game 38-26, but the two teams had a rematch seven days later in Iowa City before the largest crowd to ever see a Big Ten game to date—13,200. Lambert's tetanus had become more serious in the interim. His eyes were nearly swollen shut from a case of the hives, and he reportedly gave his pregame pep talk for the game in Iowa City from a bathtub.

He managed to make an appearance on the bench, but found the itching unbearable. The Hawkeye faithful, unaware of Lambert's medical ailment, laughed whenever Lambert would interrupt his confrontations with the referees with a scratching fit.

Ward "Piggy" Lambert

This time, however, the Boilermakers left with the scratch by beating the Hawkeyes 45-33 en route to a Big Ten title.

Death in the Locker Room

S hortly after practice on Saturday, September 12, 1936, the tired Boilermaker football team headed off to the showers. The season opener against Ohio University was two weeks away, but the difficulty of preseason drills was still on the faces of the players as they undressed. Purdue was holding drills at the Ross Camp about 10 miles to the west of campus.

Most of the players had completed their showers, but about 15 or 20 remained. In those days, players removed sticky adhesive tape from their bodies by using gasoline. It was standard practice used to soften the adhesive on the tape in order to remove it a little less painfully.

One of the shower drains was clogged, and the gasoline that washed off the players' bodies formed a thin film on top of the burgeoning water in the shower. A hard-coal water heater stood in one corner of the shower house, and the rising water level brought the gasoline to the stove. Many of the players in the showers took heed of the warning and got out of the water when the stove's initial puff blew open a small door.

There were several who had had their feet burned, but they remedied the situation by jumping directly into the Ross Camp pool adjacent to the shower facility.

What followed were bigger flames. The fire was largely confined to the floor, but in the scramble to elude the fire, six of the players fell into the fiery water. They were badly burned, but each still managed into jump in the pool.

But the damage was done for Carl Dahlbeck and Tom McGannon. They both died from complications suffered from the burns. Pat Malaska, who went on to star on the basketball team under Piggy Lambert, was one of the four survivors. So was John Drake, who went on to have an All-Star season at fullback.

Somehow, Coach Noble Kizer and the Boilermakers put the pain of the horrible incident behind them and salvaged a 5-2-1 season. Kizer, who was suffering the early stages of a kidney ailment that would later take his life, coached his final football season under the dark cloud of the terrible tragedy.

Piggy was a Cabbie

Basketball coach Ward "Piggy" Lambert loved to play poker at the old Elks Club at the corner of Fifth and Columbia streets in downtown Lafayette. Accounts vary as to whether Lambert enjoyed much success at the game, but his passion turned into an early-afternoon ritual before he held basketball practice.

In the mid-1930s, Lambert had three players who even benefited from Lambert's daily habit. Jewel Young, Johnny Sines and Pat Malaska, nicknamed by Lambert "The Three Musketeers," lived in Lafayette and spent all their time outside of classes and practice on the east side of the Wabash River.

As many did during the 1930s, when nearly all students didn't have cars, the trio made their way around town by hitchhiking. Lambert's card-playing schedule got to be so predictable that Young, Sines and Malaska knew exactly when to make their way down to the Wabash River bridge for a ride back to campus with their coach.

"I don't know if Piggy ever caught on to the fact we knew he was playing cards all the time," recalled Young, an All-American in 1938. "It was great for us, though, because we were able to count on him for a lift like clockwork."

Did He Eat Eskimo Pie?

"Piggy" Lambert loathed the rule change prior to the 1937-38 season that implemented the 10-second center line in basketball.

The reason for the rule change was because teams were stalling, which lowered the scores and made the game a yawner for fans to watch. The Boilermaker mentor, however, thought the defensive team was usually responsible for the stall tactics and did not think the rule would change things for the betterment of the game.

With the Boilermakers on their way to their 10th conference title in a home game against Illinois, Lambert got a chance to prove his point. The visiting Fighting Illini were outmanned because their star player, future baseball Hall of Famer Lou Boudreau, had been ruled ineligible after accepting $300 from the Cleveland Indians to help support his mother. Illinois was content to lay back in a zone in an effort to keep the game close.

Lambert, clinging to a 20-11 lead early in the second half, instructed his team to hold the ball. And hold it they did for the next 14 minutes.

At first, the crowd booed and threw coins on the floor. As legend has it, senior guard Pat Malaska gave the coins he had picked up to referee Dutch Clarno, offering the official an even split of proceeds. They ended up making about five bucks apiece.

During the nearly 15-minute live "intermission," Malaska also reportedly ate an Eskimo Pie while sitting on the basketball on the Fieldhouse court. When asked years later, Malaska, who had concessions rights to help pay for school in the days before athletic scholarships, stood by his story. Teammate Jewel Young, however, claimed the Eskimo Pie story was more fiction than fact.

The impasse on the basketball court finally ended when Young found an Illini defender loafing and whipped a pass to Tom Dickinson that was fumbled out of bounds. The visitors, however, had little time to change the outcome. The Boilermakers held on for a 23-13 win.

For the time being, Lambert had proven his point. It was the defense that caused play to slow down.

Noble Kizer

Aptly Named

Noble Kizer could not have had a more appropriate name. He truly was noble.

One of the "Watchcharm Guards" for the famed Four Horsemen of Notre Dame, Kizer served five years of football coaching apprenticeship at Purdue before succeeding Coach James Phelan after the Boilermakers' only undisputed title season in 1929.

Phelan and Kizer may have shared some of the same football theories, but they varied widely in their demeanor. Phelan was known as a "tough Irishman" who spoke what was on his mind and had a sharp tongue. Sarcasm was Phelan's friend.

Kizer, on the other hand, was a thinking man's coach. A talented basketball player in his day, Kizer was small but very quick. He coached football that way. He recruited players who had some of the same attributes.

"Nobe," as he was called by everyone, was friendly first, but well capable of being the boss. Kizer liked a more wide-open offense and was one of the first in the college game to substitute freely.

Not surprisingly, success followed Kizer. His first four teams at Purdue from 1930 to 1933 were an amazing 29-4-2, the best four-year stretch by any Boilermaker football coach in school history by a long shot. He was respected nationally, as he was tabbed by a vote of fans as the first coach of the College All-Star team that competed against the NFL champion in the summer game in 1934.

But it ended all too soon for Kizer. Strapped with a kidney ailment, Kizer quit football coaching to become athletics director after the 1936 season. He oversaw the building of the Purdue Fieldhouse (now known as Lambert Fieldhouse), which opened in 1938. But his health problems got the best of him, and he died at the young age of 40.

Johnny Needed Counseling

John Wooden's ambition was to become a civil engineer when he enrolled at Purdue in the fall of 1928. There were no athletic scholarships during Wooden's college days (1928-32), and the Martinsville, Indiana, native did not realize at the time that he had to go to civil engineering summer camp to be admitted into Purdue's CE school.

In those days, students didn't receive much, if any, academic counseling. Wooden was enrolled for a semester before he learned of the "summer camp" rule. So he switched his major to English, only to find out during his junior year that the state of Indiana had instituted a law that stated all coaches must have a physical education degree. Purdue, which did not have a PE degree at the time, immediately put a school in its curriculum. Certain he wanted to have the option to coach after graduation, Wooden took enough electives in PE to get his degree.

After commencement, Wooden seriously entertained offers to work in Purdue's department of English. There was no professional basketball at the time, so after much thought he decided to "barnstorm" with a semiprofessional team while pursuing work as a teacher and coach.

Wooden never lost his love for the English language. He has written a great deal of poetry and wrote daily love letters to his wife, Nell.

It Was Far from Christmas Cheer for Wooden

Three-time All-American John Wooden had his share of misfortunes off the court as a Boilermaker. Wooden spent every Christmas Day during his years at Purdue in the hospital.

His most serious calamity occurred his sophomore year of 1929-30 when he was hit by a truck on the way to the Lafayette train station to join his teammates for a trip to Indianapolis to play Butler.

The driver of a cleaning truck recognized Wooden and a teammate and motioned for the pair to jump on the back of the vehicle for a ride across the river. In snowy, icy conditions, Wooden had a hard time getting proper footing to leap on board, which subsequently forced the driver to slow down. Another truck, unable to stop from behind, nearly crushed Wooden's leg as the two vehicles collided. It was enough to put Wooden in the hospital, and he saw his playing career flash before his eyes.

"Mr. [Coach Ward "Piggy"] Lambert [the way Wooden still addresses his head coach] was not very happy with me, because we ended up losing the game to Butler," Wooden recalled. The Boilermakers recovered, however, as they went on to win the Big Ten title.

The other years spent in the infirmary? As a freshman, Wooden had scarlet fever, and as a junior, he tore a "hunk of meat" as Wooden called it, out of his hip when crashing into the bleacher after a loose ball. To cap off his college career, as a senior, Wooden thought it would be prudent to spend the holidays having his tonsils removed.

Caught on a Walk

Boilermaker basketball coach Ward "Piggy" Lambert, assistant coach Mel Taube and trainer Lon Mann made it a habit to go on a daily walk when the team was on the road. On a trip to Madison, Wisconsin, in the early 1940s, a quartet of players decided they were going to have a little fun while the coaches and the trainer were away.

The players were in cahoots with Mann, who would tip them off to Lambert's path, allowing them a little time to find a local tavern to get some beer to take back to the hotel room.

Mann usually walked a little ahead so that Taube and Lambert could have some private time. On this particular cold day in Madison, Lambert changed his path and decided to head into the tavern that the players just happened to be visiting. Luckily for the players, Mann was able to provide enough advance notice so they could hide under the table during Lambert's cameo appearance.

After Lambert left, the boys grabbed a six-pack to go and beat Lambert's posse back to the team hotel. Lambert, who had a hunch something was up, broke in on the players during a card-playing session later that evening and suspended them for the first half of the game against the Badgers.

"Had we not had beer in the room, I am not sure that Coach Lambert would not have joined in the card game," remembered Charlie "Red" Caress, one of the four guilty parties.

Paving the Way for the Hoosiers' NCAA Titles

Purdue closed out the 1939-40 basketball season with a 34-31 comeback road win over Illinois, allowing it to win the last of its 11 Big Ten titles under Coach Ward "Piggy" Lambert. The Boilermakers had been beaten by Indiana two days earlier and desperately needed a win over Illinois to capture the undisputed conference crown.

Now the question was, would Purdue accept an invitation to play in the two-year-old, eight-team NCAA Tournament? Lambert, who didn't like postseason play, said no. The coach's belief was that the 20-game season was long enough. When the NCAA asked Lambert and Boilermaker officials for their final answer on the subject, Lambert and athletics director Noble Kizer reportedly went so far as to recommend Indiana for the fledgling tournament.

Indiana, under Coach Branch McCracken, made the most of the invitation and went on to defeat Kansas for the national title.

In a situation vaguely similar to one 37 years earlier, it was Purdue's on-court play that had a role in helping the Hoosiers win the 1987 national title. Purdue's inability to clinch the Big Ten title outright in a blowout loss at Michigan helped pave the way for Indiana's championship run. Due in part to the magnitude of the Boilermakers' loss to the Wolverines, an embarrassing 104-68 defeat, the Hoosiers were awarded the opportunity to play the first four games of the NCAA Tournament in Indianapolis and Cincinnati. Hordes of Indiana fans were at both venues, making the Hoosiers feel very much at home.

It is a sore spot for the Purdue faithful to contemplate that their team's actions on and off the court played a major role in two of Indiana's five men's basketball national championships.

Marines Land at Purdue

In the summer of 1943, World War II was in full swing. The tide slowly was turning for the Allies in Europe and the Pacific, but it was taking huge numbers of American men to feed the war effort.

College enrollments were decreasing, and about half of the schools suspended their football programs. Purdue was one of the universities used as a training ground. The army refused to let its enlisted men who were on campus training play intercollegiate sports, but the marines and navy had no such restriction.

Purdue took 26 marines, nine navy men and nine civilians to field its 1943 football team. The "new" Boilermakers included linemen Alex Agase and Lou DeFilipo, All-Americans the year before at Illinois and Fordham. Babe Dimancheff, a standout at Butler, and fullback Tony Butkovich, who like Agase came from Illinois, instantly gave Purdue a powerful backfield.

Butkovich and the Boilermakers went through the first seven games in startling fashion. Coach Elmer Burnham's team, which was 1-8 the year before, jumped to as high as No. 2 in the rankings, outscoring opponents 193-48. But after the seventh game, a 32-0 win at Wisconsin, the Boilermakers had a sad ride home.

Butkovich, who had gained 973 yards and scored 16 touchdowns, and many of his fellow "trainers," had to say goodbye. It was a ride filled with many tears.

Purdue concluded its undefeated season by limping home with close victories over Minnesota and Indiana and subsequently fell to fourth in the final polls.

Alex Agase

Agase returned from the war to finish his career in style at Illinois. He later enjoyed a lengthy coaching career that included stints as the top man at Northwestern and Purdue.

Butkovich was not so lucky. He died in service to his country less than two years later.

The Ultimate Sacrifice

All-American fullback Tony Butkovich played a major role in Purdue's undefeated 1943 season.

The five-foot-11, 190-pound St. David, Illinois, native helped the Boilermakers to a 9-0 record, during which Purdue outscored its opponents 214-55.

Butkovich played for the Boilermakers for just one season. After not playing much at Illinois in 1941 and 1942, he was a V-12 transfer to Purdue under the naval lend-lease program that also included marines. The three-sport athlete from Lewistown Community High School, who ran the 100-yard dash between 9.9 and 10.0, was sent to Purdue to participate in a marine training program, a common practice in wartime.

Butkovich made the ultimate sacrifice in World War II. The 24-year-old Marine corporal was one of more than 292,000 American casualties.

The "Battering Ram" or "Chunky Illinois Express," as Butkovich was often called, was practically unstoppable on the gridiron. He romped across goal lines 16 times. Despite missing the final two Big Ten games of the 1943 season, Butkovich scored 78 points (13 touchdowns), breaking the record of 72 set 21 years earlier by Iowa's Gordon Locke. Butkovich's mark stood for 24 years.

Butkovich led the Big Ten in rushing in 1943 with 629 yards on 95 carries, a whopping 6.6 average.

In his final game, October 30 against Wisconsin, Butkovich scored three touchdowns in a 32-0 victory. Following that victory, Butkovich was told to report for Marine duty. The Wisconsin game was also the final contest of the season for teammates Alex Agase, Jimmy Darr, John Genis, Tom Hughes, Bill Newell and Bill O'Keefe. Butkovich, however, was the only known war casualty from the team.

Butkovich was a unanimous selection to the Big Ten coaches' All-Star team after having four 100-plus yard games in his brief Purdue career. His best rushing output came against Illinois on

October 2, when he had 12 carries for 207 yards.

A No. 1 draft pick of the Cleveland Rams in 1944, Butkovich was in service to his country when word of the NFL selection made its way to him. In November of 1943, he was transferred for boot training to Parris Island, South Carolina, where he became known as "Rugged Buck." After a couple more transfers, Butkovich was shipped overseas and stationed at Guadalcanal until the invasion of Okinawa.

His last official game was called "The Mosquito Bowl," which was played in Guadalcanal by two pickup Marine Corps teams on Christmas Eve 1944. The 4th and 29th marine regiments battled to a 0-0 tie.

The Okinawa landing began at 8:30 a.m. on April 1 (Easter Sunday), 1945. Butkovich, a mortar man who was a member of the 3rd Battalion, 29th Regiment, 6th Division, was killed April 18, 1945, by a nocturnal sniper during fighting on the Motobu peninsula.

In Butkovich's obituary, he was called "One of Purdue's Greatest."

The campaign for Okinawa ended July 2. For the United States, it had been the longest and bloodiest Pacific battle since Guadalcanal in 1942. It cost 12,000 American lives, while another 36,000 were wounded.

Butkovich was buried on Okinawa and laid to rest there until his mother, Anna, had his body returned home June 16, 1949. He is now buried in Canton (Illinois) Cemetery.

The Cradle
Started in Dayton

Not only did Bob DeMoss coach many of the great Boilermaker quarterbacks from Dale Samuels to Gary Danielson, but his playing career is considered the genesis of

Purdue's "Cradle of Quarterbacks."

DeMoss came to Purdue from Dayton, Kentucky, in the summer of 1945. He played on the first Kentucky All-Star basketball team to defeat Indiana in its annual summer series and was courted by the University of Kentucky's legendary basketball coach Adolph Rupp.

After the Kentucky stars defeated Indiana in Butler's fieldhouse, Rupp came racing over to DeMoss on the court and asked the high school senior to join him in Lexington for the next four years with budding stars Ralph Beard and Wah Jones. Rupp laid it on thick with DeMoss, but not thick enough to close the deal at that moment.

Waiting for DeMoss in the locker room was Boilermaker head football coach Cecil Isbell. In the middle of the summer, Isbell was dressed fashionably in a summer hat and didn't have too much to say except to affirm that DeMoss still was interested in Purdue.

DeMoss not only was interested, he was ready to say yes to Isbell.

Beard and Jones went on to win a pair of NCAA basketball titles and Olympic gold medals at Kentucky, not bad careers to say the least. DeMoss, who played on the Boilermakers' freshman basketball team, wasted little time making an impact on the gridiron. He shocked the college football world by beating No. 4 Ohio State 35-13 in his fifth college game as a true freshman. He left Purdue as the school's all-time leading passer and had a perfect record against the Buckeyes.

DeMoss's life would have been different had he given into Rupp. So would have the story of Purdue football. He will go down in college football history as one of the great quarterback coaches of all time. Just ask Len Dawson, Bob Griese and Mike Phipps.

Rare Rankings

Purdue and Indiana have met on the football field 105 times through the 2002 season. Since 1891, the Boilermakers and Hoosiers have played every year except 1895, 1896, 1903, 1906, 1907, 1918 and 1919. Only eight rivalries in the country have a longer duration.

Yet only one game in the series history has taken place when both teams were nationally ranked in the Associated Press poll, which debuted in 1936.

The date was November 24, 1945, and the No. 4 Hoosiers shut out the No. 18 Boilermakers 26-0 at the original Memorial Stadium in Bloomington. Ironic, perhaps, since World War II had ended in August.

Both Purdue and Indiana had been in the Big Ten championship hunt until the Boilermakers lost at Michigan 27-13 the week before the battle for the Old Oaken Bucket. It left the Hoosiers in the driver's seat, needing only to beat their rivals from the north. After a scoreless first half, Indiana rolled in the final 30 minutes to capture their first-ever conference crown before a capacity-plus crowd of nearly 27,000, including 4,000 veterans.

The Boilermakers finished 7-3 overall and 3-3 in the Big Ten for a fourth-place tie with Wisconsin. They were not ranked in the final AP poll.

No Money, but Lots of Fun

When Dave Rankin returned from World War II to coach at Purdue in 1946, he was hired by athletics director Red Mackey to coach the track and field team and assist with the freshman football squad. Mackey's sales pitch wasn't one that knocked Rankin's socks off, but he was impressed with

Red's honesty.

"You won't make any money here, but we'll have a lot of fun," Mackey said.

Mackey got the money part right, at least in the early years. Rankin's starting salary was $3,200 per year. According to Rankin, Mackey got the fun part right, as well.

Winning Rub

Football placekickers are known for utilizing strange rituals in hopes that they will help them make those big kicks. But it is not often that one hears of a holder doing something a little unique.

Purdue was playing the Pitt Panthers in Pittsburgh on October 26, 1946, and the defensive struggle left the visitors trailing 8-7 in the closing minute of the fourth quarter. The call came down from Coach Cecil Isbell, who managed the game from the press box, to assistant Joe Dienhart to send kicker Hank Stram into the game to attempt the game-winning field goal.

When Stram ran into the huddle, holder Johnny Galvin grabbed Stram's right foot and pulled his boot off. He started rubbing Stram's toes right on the field in the huddle. Stram thought Galvin was going to break his ankle, he was rubbing so hard.

"Hank, we gotta make this kick, we just gotta," Galvin said as he rubbed away. Stram, who never had experienced anything quite like this on a football field, responded with the game-winning kick. Purdue left Pittsburgh with a hard-fought 10-8 win, and Stram left wondering if he should ask his teammate for a pedicure on the ride home.

Hank Stram

Coaches on the Field

The 1946 football team featured four players who went on to become college and/or professional head coaches.

Quarterback Bob DeMoss coached the Boilermakers from 1970 to 1972.

Guard Abe Gibron was with the Chicago Bears from 1972 to 1974.

Reserve back John McKay coached at USC from 1960 to 1975 (including the 1967 Rose Bowl against the Boilermakers) and later was the first coach of the expansion Tampa Bay Buccaneers from 1976 to 1984.

Kicker and reserve back Hank Stram was head coach of the Dallas Texans and Kansas City Chiefs from 1960 to 1974 (winning Super Bowl IV) and later with the New Orleans Saints in 1976 and 1977.

Despite all those coaches on the field, the 1946 Boilermakers managed just a 2-6-1 record in Cecil Isbell's final season as coach. Ironically, Isbell also became a professional coach. He left Purdue to coach the Baltimore Colts in the fledgling All-American Football Conference in 1947. He coached the Colts for nearly three seasons.

Lethal Crash at the Fieldhouse

Purdue's on-court struggles during the 1946-47 basketball season became instantly insignificant the night of February 24, 1947, at the Purdue Fieldhouse. The Boilermakers were playing host to Big Nine leader Wisconsin in front of an overflow crowd of 11,000. Thanks to 11 points by All-American Paul "The Bear" Hoffman, Purdue clung to a one-point lead as the Boilermaker faithful roared as their team left the court for intermission.

Less than one minute later, tragedy struck.

Screams of horror were heard from the jam-packed east bleachers. Before anyone could realize what was happening, the bleachers, less than a year old and taken from the football stadium, shifted forward and fell toward the floor in a slow, accordion-like motion. The 30-foot high stands made a cracking noise as they descended.

"Voice of Purdue" John DeCamp summoned emergency help during his radio broadcast as PA announcer Jim Miles kept things calm in the Fieldhouse. From all accounts, matters were surprisingly orderly as the search began through the rubble. Volunteers used the fractured bleachers as stretchers, and the court turned into an emergency treatment area. Students William Feldman and Roger Gelhausen lay mortally wounded, as they were under the bleachers when they collapsed. Theodore Nordquist died two days later from injuries sustained. In all, 300 fans were admitted to local hospitals.

A formal investigation, led by Indiana Gov. Ralph Gates, determined that structural failure was to blame. Because the Badgers were in the title chase, the two teams, who were sent home at halftime, finished the game two weeks later at Evanston (Illinois) Township High School. Wisconsin rallied for a 72-60 win and won the conference crown—its last in the 20th century. Not surprisingly, the Boilermakers' hearts were not in the game.

Holcomb Learns His Lesson

In his first season as head football coach, Stuart Holcomb's 1947 squad upset Ohio State 24-20 on October 4 en route to a 5-4 season. But the Boilermakers lost their annual finale to intrastate rival Indiana 16-14 on November 22. It was their fourth straight loss to Indiana, and the natives were growing restless.

Being a newcomer to the rivalry, Holcomb didn't understand what all the fuss was about. "We didn't put that much importance on the Indiana game," he admitted. "We actually believed that when we upset Ohio State we gave our fans a successful season. But if victory over Indiana is what they want, that's what they'll get. Indiana never will beat us again."

Pretty heady talk, to be sure, but Holcomb was true to his word. He coached the Boilermakers for eight more seasons and beat the Hoosiers eight times.

Among Purdue grid bosses, only Jack Mollenkopf has beaten Indiana more often than Holcomb, with 11 wins in 14 meetings from 1956 to 1969.

Don't Care for the "White Hats"

Under Piggy Lambert, Purdue was known by many as the best basketball team in the "West." That was true especially in the 1920s and '30s, when Purdue was winning conference titles at a minimum of every other year.

Several times during Lambert's nearly three-decade run as the Boilermakers' head coach, his teams traveled to distant locales to play games.

In those days, Purdue played on both coasts, but Lambert developed a dislike for playing in the Big Apple. He did not like the atmosphere surrounding New York's famed Madison Square Garden. The "white hats," the label he used for gamblers, were much too evident for his comfort.

Piggy proclaimed during a trip to New York in 1935 that one day the "white hats" would make shambles of college basketball. Much like everything else in the game, Lambert was far ahead of his time. About 15 years later, City College of New York (CCNY) was implicated in a point-shaving scandal that set the college basketball world on its ear.

CHAPTER 2

1950s

Moose Was a Piece of Work

R ay "Cracker" Schalk, who is enshrined in the Baseball Hall of Fame in Cooperstown, New York, served for 16 years as an assistant baseball coach at Purdue.

As a member of Hank Stram's coaching staff, he recruited Bill "Moose" Skowron out of the Chicago area. Skowron had made a name for himself as a power hitter, partly on the strength of being able to hit a softball over the fence at Wrigley Field. He also was a pretty fair football player, serving as the Boilermakers' punter during the 1949 season.

Skowron only played one year at Purdue before signing with the New York Yankees for an astounding $25,000 bonus. After he signed with New York, he was asked by Stram to serve as a guest speaker at one of Stram's classes.

Stram thought Skowron could relay the thought process he used when making the decision to leave Purdue for professional baseball. When asked by students in the class why he left Purdue, his answer came out a little differently than Stram expected.

"I wasn't doing much at Purdue," said Skowron, who batted .293 in eight World Series appearances with the Bronx Bombers and was inducted into the Purdue Intercollegiate Athletics Hall of Fame in 1996. "I was playing a lot of pool and ping pong at the fraternity house and I wasn't going to class very much, so why wouldn't I leave?"

"That was classic Moose," Stram recalled. "It wasn't exactly what I wanted him to say, but at least he was honest."

Wizard Walks Away

John Wooden, who coached UCLA to 10 national championships in 12 years, was twice considered for the Purdue head basketball coaching job.

After Piggy Lambert resigned during the middle of the 1946 season, Mel Taube finished out the year as acting head coach, posting a 3-4 record. The Boilermakers' eighth-place conference finish was their worst in 30 years, but Taube was given the full-time job thanks to a petition signed by the players and given to president Frederick Hovde.

Accounts vary whether Wooden was approached by Purdue officials for the job at the time Taube was given the full-time opportunity. After the end of World War II, Wooden headed for his first college coaching position at Indiana State, where he won 75 percent of his games before heading to UCLA prior to the 1948-49 season.

According to Wooden, Purdue privately asked him to stay at Indiana State for the 1948-49 season and then move to West Lafayette at season's end. Purdue then would replace Taube, who was not winning popularity contests at Purdue, with Wooden. That scenario, however, did not sit well with Wooden, who did not like the idea of putting Taube in the position of being a "lame duck."

The following year, Purdue came calling again. Taube had been fired as head coach, and Boilermaker athletics director Red Mackey offered the job to Wooden. The story around Greater Lafayette was that Wooden had agreed to be the Purdue coach—at least for three days. Wooden was on the East Coast conducting a basketball clinic and called his wife, Nell, to inform her that they were moving to Indiana. Nell reportedly did not want to leave her new home and newly made friends in Los Angeles. Instead of stopping in West Lafayette on his way home, Wooden flew directly to Los Angeles. Wooden then called Mackey and said he would honor his "72-hour agreement" with Mackey, but Mackey said he did not want Wooden if his heart and soul weren't in the Purdue job.

A wire service story on April 1, 1950, stated that Wooden wanted his name off the Purdue list and reported that his three-year deal at UCLA, for a whopping $8,000 annually, was increased to an unprecedented $12,000 per year for the next 10 seasons.

Six days later, Ray Eddy, who played with Wooden in his sophomore year at Purdue, was named the Boilermaker head coach. Amazingly, Eddy just had been hired as a high school coach in Kokomo, Indiana, a few weeks earlier. He took a $500 pay cut to come to Purdue.

Wooden Dislikes Nickname

John Wooden has carried the nickname "The Wizard of Westwood" since the days of UCLA's reign of college basketball in the 1960s and '70s.

Surprisingly, Wooden never has liked the moniker. He believed the title evolved out of spite from members of the media who didn't care for him. Their dislike stemmed from Wooden not allowing sportswriters in the locker room after games.

"I always believed the players deserved their privacy and that they should be able to shower and get dressed without a bunch of strangers hanging around," Wooden said.

People Everywhere

Purdue traveled to Notre Dame Stadium on a drizzly day on October 7, 1950, with the hopes of ending the Fighting Irish's 39-game unbeaten string. The Irish, under Coach Frank Leahy, had been unbeatable since the 1945 season.

The Boilermakers had come within a point of stopping the streak two years earlier in a 28-27 loss, but this time they left little doubt. They jumped out to a 21-0 first-half lead thanks to the play of sophomore quarterback Dale Samuels and receivers Bernie Flowers, Mike Maccioli and Neil Schmidt.

The second half got bumpy at times as the Irish cut the lead to 21-14, but Samuels hit Schmidt for a 56-yard scoring pass and the Boilermakers were home free.

Well, not exactly.

When Purdue returned to Lafayette after the game, they were greeted at the Big Four Train Station downtown with a crowd so large that the mile-long-plus bus trip back to campus was wall-to-wall people.

Those who witnessed the event say the only bigger celebration the city has ever seen was after the Japanese surrendered to end World War II. President Frederick Hovde held an impromptu pep session at the Hall of Music that over 6,000 fans attended and promptly called off school. The Boilermaker celebration and ending of the Irish's streak even was featured in *Life* magazine.

Surprisingly, the 1950 team only managed one other win during the season—a 13-0 shutout of Indiana in the final game of the season. It will go down as the team that got the most out of two victories in the program's history.

Hooray for Hollywood

Thanks, in part, to Hollywood, Len Dawson discovered Purdue.

Believing the school was somewhere in Illinois, Dawson, an Alliance, Ohio, native, was at the movies one night when a Movietone newsreel showing clips of Purdue's 28-14 upset over No. 1 Notre Dame on October 7, 1950, which ended the Irish's 39-game unbeaten streak, was shown before the feature presentation. The newsreel also showed halfback Mike Maccioli scoring a pair of touchdowns. Dawson became even more

Len Dawson

interested in Purdue since Maccioli was from his high school.

Dawson was lured to West Lafayette by the way Coach Stuart Holcomb ran his offense. At that time most schools ran the split-T offense, emphasizing the run. Purdue had a more pass-oriented offense.

"I wouldn't have been successful in the split-T," said Dawson, who was recruited by Ohio State and Notre Dame among others. "I was fortunate that I was a passing quarterback in high school. Purdue was one of the few schools in the country that threw the football."

Dawson's decision to go to Purdue paid big dividends. He set school career records for touchdown passes with 29 and passing yardage with 3,319. Dawson continued his success at the highest level. He was a first-round pick of the Pittsburgh Steelers in the 1957 draft, selected over Jim Brown, and went on to be one of pro football's best quarterbacks. Dawson won four AFL passing titles and established Kansas City Chiefs records for completions, passing yards and touchdown passes. He helped the Chiefs win Super Bowl IV and was named the game's Most Valuable Player.

Lenny Makes a Choice and Keeps a Secret

Quarterback Len Dawson made a couple fateful decisions during his senior year in high school. First the Alliance, Ohio, native bucked the locals by choosing to attend Purdue over Ohio State.

"[Ohio State legendary coach] Woody Hayes told me that I could come to Ohio State, but I would not start until I was a junior," Dawson said. "It was kind of like they wanted me, but they were not sure I could do the job or not."

Purdue was sure Dawson could do the job and was eager to get him on campus. Just weeks before leaving eastern Ohio for central Indiana, Dawson made another important decision. He married his high school sweetheart, Jackie.

The pair drove to Indiana and eloped. Jackie returned home to Alliance to live with her parents without telling them she was married. Dawson started his freshman year with the secret in tow.

The secret was safe for a couple of months until Jackie became pregnant. She moved to Lafayette with her new husband the following May, two months after their daughter was born.

To help Dawson make it through school, Purdue assistant football coach Hank Stram, whose father-in-law owned a local grocery store, delivered groceries to the prized quarterback who had a family to feed. It was the genesis of a long-lasting relationship that landed both in the Pro Football Hall of Fame.

Purdue's "Golden Boy"

Len Dawson didn't waste any time making a name for himself at Purdue.

In his first two collegiate games in 1954, he passed for eight touchdowns against Missouri and Notre Dame. His Boilermaker debut came against the Tigers. The Alliance, Ohio, native entered the game as a reserve and threw four scoring strikes in the 31-0 win. In his second game, four of his seven completions were touchdowns, helping Purdue to a 27-14 victory over the top-ranked Irish.

Dawson was nicknamed "The Golden Boy" by the media following those two memorable performances. As a result, a few years later, the Purdue "All-American" Marching Band developed "The Golden Girl."

Paying Back
the Spartans Times Two

The year 1953 was the best of times for Michigan State. It was, in terms of wins and losses, one of the worst of times for Purdue.

Coach Biggie Munn's Spartans were riding a 28-game winning streak and seemed poised to make easy work of the Boilermakers in Ross-Ade Stadium. Purdue entered the game reeling from an 0-4 start. After gaining a share of the Big Ten championship the year before, the Boilermakers had fallen into the Big Ten's basement.

It was an unresolved issue from that title season, however, that would provide, at least in the Boilermakers' minds, some of the impetus for one of the greatest college football upsets of the 1950s.

Purdue shared the 1952 crown with Wisconsin, but had not played the Badgers. There were many who thought the Boilermakers deserved the trip to Pasadena. After all, Stu Holcomb's team had played a murderous non-conference schedule that included a tie at Penn State, a close loss to No. 1 Michigan State (the Spartans did not officially begin Big Ten play until 1953) and a defeat at the hands of Notre Dame. In a close vote of conference athletic directors, it was thought that Michigan State and Ohio State were swing votes that both tabbed the Badgers over Purdue.

The Purdue camp had not forgotten the perceived snub and went on to play the game of the year against the Spartans. The Boilermakers' new 4-5-2 defensive scheme caught Michigan State off guard as Purdue intercepted five passes.

With the game still scoreless late in the third quarter, Purdue embarked on the game-winning drive. A roughing-the-punter penalty at midfield kept the drive alive that set the stage for some personal payback to the Spartans.

Fullback Dan Pobojewski, who in essence had been cut from Michigan State's football team three years earlier, carried the ball into the end zone for the game's only touchdown. A native of Jackson, Michigan, "Pobo" was so emotional after scoring that he wept as he ran back to the bench shielding his face from teammates so that his tears would go unnoticed.

After the dramatic 6-0 win, the Boilermakers returned to earth, losing three of their final four games. Still, that victory over the Green and White remains one of the most memorable upsets in an era when Purdue football was known for upsetting some of college football's powerhouses.

Overtime Stalled Out

It wasn't that Coach Ray Eddy's Boilermakers lost the longest game in Big Ten history—a six-overtime affair to Minnesota in West Lafayette on January 29, 1955—that rubbed him the wrong way.

It was how they lost it.

The score was knotted at 47 after the regulation 40 minutes. In the 30 minutes that followed, Minnesota outscored Purdue 12-9 to pull off the 59-56 victory in a game marred by stalling by both teams.

In the first four overtime periods, neither team scored as Purdue was the only team to attempt a field goal. The Boilermakers failed to convert any of their shots in the closing seconds of the first trio of extra periods. In the fifth overtime, Boilermaker standout Joe Sexson broke the prolonged dry spell with a field goal, but Minnesota answered. With three seconds left, Sexson fired from behind the foul circle. The shot appeared to be good, but Minnesota's six-foot-11, 275-pound center, Bill Simonovich, put his hand through the bottom of the net and knocked the ball out. For some reason, the under official, whose only responsibility is the action in front of him, overruled the out official's goaltending call. Eddy erupted and had to be restrained by assistant coach Joe Dienhart.

The pace picked up in the sixth extra period. Purdue managed to forge a pair of three-point leads. But three crucial turnovers in the game's final 3:26 gave Minnesota the win.

The loss was devastating to Eddy, who was desperately trying to turn around the once-proud Boilermaker basketball program. After four losing seasons to begin his tenure at Purdue, his squad showed much promise in 1954-55. It began the season 8-1 and leaped to a No. 17 national ranking—the first time his program had been ranked. The Boilermakers did get their elusive winning season with a 12-10 record, but the six-overtime loss threw a wet blanket on a promising year.

Did the Press Pitch In?

When Coach Stu Holcomb left the Purdue football team after the 1955 season to become athletic director at Northwestern, Purdue athletics director Red Mackey was left with a tough decision on whom to hire. Holcomb and Mackey's relationship had deteriorated toward the end of Holcomb's tenure, but there were several talented assistant coaches who warranted Mackey's consideration for the job opening.

Jack Mollenkopf and fellow assistant coach Hank Stram were two of the men thought best suited for the opening.

A line coach who believed in defense first, Mollenkopf was given the job, much to the delight of *Lafayette Journal and Courier* sports editor Gordon Graham. The newspaper played a very powerful role at the time and had the ear of President Frederick Hovde and Mackey. There are some who say Graham's influence with Purdue played a major role in getting Mollenkopf the job.

Whatever the case, Mollenkopf made the most of the opportunity, going on to become the school's all-time winningest coach in a span from 1956 to 1969.

Jack Mollenkopf

Coach Turned Shipbuilder

H e really wanted to be a football coach, but his dad wanted him to run the family business.

George Steinbrenner served as a volunteer assistant coach during Jack Mollenkopf's first season as head coach at Purdue in 1956. He did the same thing at Northwestern.

No sports figure in the 20th century hated losing more than Steinbrenner. But the fact that the Boilermakers finished with a

3-4-2 record in 1956 had nothing to do with him leaving Purdue and ultimately changing careers.

It was quite the contrary. Steinbrenner's father, George II, called his son back to run the family business. The father and son had a difficult relationship. George was always trying to live up to dad's expectations. The opportunity to run the family business was more mandatory than voluntary. When his father called, Steinbrenner had little choice but to heed the call.

Working in the family business, Steinbrenner earned his fortune by heading the Cleveland-based American Shipbuilding Company.

His connection with Purdue remained after he left the Boilermaker campus. He provided numerous summer jobs to Boilermaker athletes prior to becoming principal owner of the New York Yankees in 1973. Under Mollenkopf, Bob DeMoss and Alex Agase, the Boilermakers found the Cleveland area fertile for cultivating talent, and Steinbrenner played a role in their success.

Coat Check

More recent fans of Boilermaker basketball recognize Gene Keady as the master of the coat toss. During the late 1990s, it seemed like an every-game occurrence that Keady would get frustrated with his team or the officials and toss his coat into the bench or, better yet, toward his wife, Pat, seated behind him.

Keady's antics, however, aren't anything new to Boilermaker basketball. Ray Eddy, who coached the Boilermakers from 1951 to 1965, had a habit of tossing his coat. That is, until he learned his lesson for good.

Former Big Ten official Jimmy Enright was getting on Eddy's nerves in a game at "The Barn" in Minnesota. Coaches are seated below the floor at the Golden Gophers' facility with fans bumped up right behind the team. Eddy argued another call of Enright's and hopped onto the four-step ladder that led to the court to get in the face of the official. After a brief discussion with Enright, Eddy was so disgusted that he flung his coat. The Boilermaker boss did not intend for it to go very far, but somehow Eddy's toss had a slingshot effect and the coat went several rows deep into the stands.

At first, Eddy wasn't in any big hurry to retrieve his coat. He probably figured the Gopher fans would eventually bring it back to the bench. Suddenly, however, Eddy remembered he had all the team's travel money in his coat pocket. Not surprisingly, the focus of his attention changed from the game and referees to the fact that there was $1,500 in his pocket.

Eddy sent managers and players into the crowd, and they retrieved the coat without further incident. Needless to say, Eddy checked his coat pocket before ever tossing his coat again.

CHAPTER 3

1960s

The Legend of John Konsek

Boilermaker golfing legend John Konsek had Jack Nicklaus's number. Well, sort of.

The legend around Purdue for years was that Konsek never lost a match to Nicklaus. The truth is, however, that Konsek and Nicklaus only competed against one another for one season in college. Though the same age, Konsek was a brilliant student who enrolled at Purdue at age 16, two years ahead of Nicklaus.

In the 1960 golf season, Konsek lost in head-to-head competition to Nicklaus in a match played at Ohio State's Scarlet Course. When the two met in West Lafayette a week later, Konsek used his knowledge of the Purdue South Course to pull off the stunning upset. In the Big Ten championships held at Michigan State's Forest Akers Course, Konsek endured the cold and rainy weather to edge Nicklaus for his still-standing record third straight Big Ten individual title.

Fellow Boilermaker Gene Francis won the medalist honors at the NCAA championships two weeks later at the windy Broadmoor course in Colorado Springs, Colorado. Nicklaus finished three strokes behind Francis, but five strokes ahead of Konsek. Nicklaus and Konsek did not face each other in the

NCAA Tournament match-play competition, as both players were eliminated before the finals.

Konsek finished second in the match-play competition to successful PGA player Phil Rodgers as a sophomore in 1958.

In a couple of his golf books, Nicklaus called Konsek one of his toughest competitors in his college days. Nicklaus wondered what kind of player Konsek would have been on the PGA Tour.

Konsek was convinced that the PGA Tour was not for him. Some friends had encouraged him to go to dental school so he would have time to keep his golf game sharp, but Konsek chose to become a physician, building a distinguished career spanning three decades in cancer medicine. He was inducted into the Purdue Intercollegiate Athletics Hall of Fame in 2003.

Bernie Brings 'Em Back Against the Bruins

B ernie Allen was one of the most talented two-sport athletes in Purdue history. A member of the Intercollegiate Athletics Hall of Fame, Allen made his name on the gridiron and baseball field. He played in the major leagues for the Washington Senators and Minnesota Twins from 1962 to 1972.

At Purdue, his summer baseball schedule sometimes caused problems with his football career. In the 1960 season opener against eighth-ranked UCLA in Ross-Ade Stadium, Allen did not start the game, reportedly because he missed too much practice due to his summer baseball commitments. After the Boilermakers fell behind 20-0, however, Coach Jack Mollenkopf inserted Allen into the lineup.

Despite the limited practice time, Allen led a rousing comeback, tossing two touchdown passes as the Boilermakers battled back to tie the Bruins at 27. Strangely, it was the second tie in as many years between the two teams. The year before at the Los Angeles Coliseum, the Boilermakers and Bruins played to a scoreless deadlock in what observers called one of the worst college football games ever played by either school.

Holiday Celebration

Purdue's trip to Notre Dame on October 1, 1960, fell on the Jewish holiday Yom Kippur. Boilermaker starting quarterback Maury Guttman, who was Jewish, was determined to make this day a special one for his teammates and himself.

At the coin toss before kickoff, Guttman met his former high school teammate and opposing team captain Myron Pottious. Despite being tagged a three-point underdog, Guttman looked at his friend, who was Catholic, and proclaimed, "We're going to beat your behind today. Today is my holiday!"

Guttman's words rang true as the Boilermakers delivered one of the great whippings ever administered to the Fighting Irish under the shadow of the golden dome. Purdue scored a school-record 45 points in the first half en route to a 51-19 win.

Sunk by the Navy

Heisman Trophy winner and NFL Hall of Fame quarterback Roger Staubach, who led the Dallas Cowboys to a pair of Super Bowl championships, committed to play at Purdue out of Cincinnati Purcell Marian High School.

"We thought at the time how great it was because we finally beat Ohio State for a talented player," recalled Bob DeMoss, whose area of recruiting responsibility included Cincinnati. The only problem was that Staubach's mother always wanted her son to be in the armed services. So instead of enrolling at Purdue, Staubach headed to New Mexico for naval prep school before entering the Naval Academy.

Winning the Title

P urdue won its first of two team national titles in school history on its home golf course on June 20, 1961. The Boilermakers had finished runner-up in the team competition, which prior to 1965 consisted of the 36 holes qualifying for match play, five times since 1949. Purdue had finished second the last two years (1959 and 1960), but this time the Boilermakers owned the home-course advantage and a good dose of good fortune.

Houston, which was riding a streak of five straight national titles, finished out of the running after one player was penalized 16 strokes for having too many clubs in his bag. In the end, the Boilermakers outdistanced Arizona State by 11 strokes for the crown thanks to two great rounds by Mark Darnell.

Ohio State's Jack Nicklaus, who had a Tiger Woods-like following on the South and North courses, edged Darnell by a stroke for medalist honors due to Darnell's double bogey on the 17th hole. Still, the combined scores of Darnell, two-time All-American Jerry Jackson, Steve Wilkinson and James Farlander were enough to give Purdue a comfortable win. Amazingly, all the Boilermakers were underclassmen, and the general consensus was that the Boilermaker program would take a pronounced dip after the 1960 Big Ten title.

Nicklaus, however, won the NCAA individual title in match play. Jackson was the highest Purdue finisher, reaching the round of 16.

Change of Delivery

T he greatest "throw-in" recruit in Purdue sports history might have to be two-time All-America quarterback Bob Griese. The Evansville, Indiana, native was the "other guy" in the derby to land the services of high school basketball standout

Bob Griese

Tom Niemeyer.

Niemeyer left Purdue just over a year after he arrived, transferring back to his hometown and the University of Evansville. Griese, who was Niemeyer's buddy and played basketball himself, was considered to be a better candidate at strong safety than at quarterback. In fact, he spent nearly two thirds of his time with the Boilermaker defense in his first spring practice in 1964.

The football coaches loved Griese's leadership but could not figure out what was wrong with his throwing motion. At the conclusion of spring ball, Griese still was in the running for the starting quarterback job, but his wobbly passes put doubts in the minds of the coaches.

Cecil Isbell, who played and coached at Purdue two decades earlier before a brief stint as head coach of the Baltimore Colts, was back visiting his former pupil and current quarterbacks coach Bob DeMoss. After having lunch, DeMoss brought Isbell back to his office to show him film on this promising but puzzling freshman quarterback.

After two plays of game film, Isbell told DeMoss to shut off the projector. He had seen enough. Isbell immediately spotted on film that Griese didn't have his right wrist positioned correctly when beginning the process of throwing the football.

"Correct that and you will correct the problem," Isbell said.

DeMoss called Griese into his office and stood him in front of a mirror. He worked with his pupil to show him the flaw and sent him on his way for the summer.

"To Bob's credit, he worked on it all summer, so much so that when he came back to campus he was ready to go," DeMoss said. "Griese was one of the hardest-working players we have ever had before he became the great leader he was."

Billy Packer Does Purdue a Big Favor

It is hard to believe that many schools didn't recruit African-American athletes as late as the mid-1960s.

One of the greatest players in Purdue men's basketball history, Herman Gilliam, enrolled at Purdue on that racist pretense and a little help from current CBS analyst Billy Packer.

Packer, a young assistant coach at Wake Forest at the time, had befriended Boilermaker assistant Bob King. Packer, who had watched Gilliam play in Winston Salem, North Carolina, the home of Wake Forest, told King about this great talent in early 1965. Wake Forest was still a couple of years away from admitting blacks to its school.

Gilliam's mother developed a bond with King and his wife, Nancy, and that factor helped him chose Purdue over Minnesota.

"Herman Gilliam was way ahead of his time as a player," King said. "He had the skills that suited the game as it is played in the 21st century. He was one of the few players that could shift his game into another gear."

A key player in the Boilermakers' trek to the Final Four in 1969, Gilliam proved to be quite a talent in the 20th century, playing 10 years in the NBA and winning a league title with the Portland Trail Blazers.

Red Mackey and Basketball

By all accounts, Red Mackey, who served as Purdue athletics director for three decades until 1971, was a football guy. He played football for the Boilermakers under Coach Jim Phelan from 1926 to 1928 and served 12 years as an assistant coach before becoming the head man in the department.

When it came to basketball, Mackey was supportive. But hoops took a back seat to football, at least in the minds of Mackey and some Boilermaker fans. Purdue did not win a conference basketball title during his first 27 years as athletics director and fell into a middle-of-the-road program for the majority of his tenure.

In 1965, when it came time for Mackey to replace Ray Eddy as basketball coach, Mackey gathered names. He told longtime assistant coaches Joe Sexson and Bob King that their jobs as assistants were secure, but they would not be considered for the head position. He wanted his own man and was looking for a surprise candidate.

With the help of Bob King, Mackey entered into discussions with George King, head coach of West Virginia. Mackey did not know much about George King. When Bob King gave him the name, Mackey half-jokingly said, "Are you trying to get your brother a job?" though the two were not related.

Mackey liked George King's honest, down-home attitude and his ability to sell. King sealed the deal with Mackey after a lengthy phone conversation between the pair.

It made Mackey especially proud a few years later when King took the Boilermakers to the national championship game. Mackey knew then that his legacy would be known for more than his ability to work with the football program. It was ironic that he went to his deathbed knowing that his name would be forever etched on a basketball palace and not a football stadium.

The Reluctant Kicker

Bob Griese always had a quiet air of confidence about him. But one area in which he had some doubts of his ability was long-distance placekicking.

Griese was a three-year starter at quarterback form 1964 to 1966, but he also handled Purdue's placekicking duties. His range was usually limited to 35 yards.

The Michigan game in 1965 found the Boilermakers trailing 15-14 with under a minute left in the contest. The junior, who already was in the huddle after a failed third-down conversion, received word from senior running back Gordon Teter that the coaching staff had called for a field goal attempt.

"I can't make one from that far," Griese reportedly said to his pal Teter in the huddle. Teter, who would go on to be CEO of Wendy's International, had a voice that was barely audible. But when he spoke, his teammates listened.

"They want you to make this field goal," Teter told Griese in a simple, matter-of-fact manner. Against a stiff wind, Griese, a straight-ahead kicker, did what he was told and made the 38-yard field goal that gave Purdue a 17-15 win in the Big House.

Griese has the distinction of being the only quarterback in college football history to defeat Michigan three consecutive years in Ann Arbor. He did it by about as slim a margin as possible—a whopping total of four points.

The Rocket Almost Swept Up by a Hurricane

P urdue probably has never had a more prolonged battle for a recruit in its athletics history than the duel to get Rick "The Rocket" Mount to West Lafayette. The first high school player ever to be featured on the cover of *Sports Illustrated*, every school in the country was interested in Mount.

A native of Lebanon, Indiana, just 40 miles southeast of the Purdue campus, Mount had pared down his college choices to Purdue and Miami (Florida). Mount initially made a well-publicized, but nonbinding in the eyes of the NCAA, commitment to attend Miami on May 17, 1966, to play for its upstart Coach Bruce Hale. The Hurricanes' boss, who had mentored NBA star Rick Barry, lured Mount with relentless pressure based in part on the promise that he would fly game film back to Lebanon. Mount knew it was important to the people of hometown to see their favorite son score every basket of his collegiate career if at all possible.

Like most teenagers would in that situation, Mount bowed to Hale's sales tactics. He agreed to commit to Miami almost to get Hale off his back. In one of the greatest displays of patience in Boilermaker basketball history, chief Boilermaker recruiter Bob King, who also happened to be a distant relative of Mount, decided to wait it out and let the Lebanon townspeople do some of the legwork for him.

"There was no way the people of Lebanon were going to allow him to go that far away to school," King recalled years after the fact. "The mayor of the town was also a relative of mine, so I was able to monitor the situation pretty darn closely."

Mount spent the summer of 1965 playing with former Boilermaker Bob Purkhiser, a spectacular shooter in his own right who became an overseas hoops star before his untimely death a few years later. King, who had recruited Purkhiser, said the two hit it off and that the relationship kept Purdue's hopes alive that Mount would change his mind.

It didn't hurt that Mount was scoring 30 to 40 points a game in pickup games with current and former Big Ten stars in contests that drew huge crowds in the Lebanon and Indianapolis areas. If Mount had any doubt that he could play in the Big Ten, he silenced it that summer.

Mount kept the Boilermaker fans and coaches waiting, however. It was August 4 before he formally announced that he had changed his mind and was going to attend Purdue.

Great Tragedy Before Great Triumph

G ary Bancroft was a basketball player with tremendous potential.

Nearly a decade before freshmen were eligible for varsity competition, the Linden, Michigan, native turned heads by scoring 21 points in the annual freshman-varsity game in November of 1965. It certainly impressed first-year coach George King.

The six-foot-six athletic forward was one of the many athletic players King had recruited in his early days at Purdue. Bancroft, who had seven brothers and sisters, was a free spirit of the 1960s, but the Boilermakers had big plans for him. That is, until July 28, 1966.

Enrolled in summer school, Bancroft was giving a demonstration on the trampoline before a physical education class. Classified by his instructors as an expert gymnast, Bancroft did a routine forward somersault and landed wrong. Terribly wrong.

He fractured his neck and was pronounced dead shortly thereafter at the student hospital. Just seven days later, the Boilermaker basketball program, still reeling from the tragedy, had learned that Rick Mount, the most coveted basketball player in America, changed his mind from a commitment to attend Miami and decided to enroll at Purdue.

Rose Bowl Mirror Image

Despite not sleeping in their own beds for nearly two weeks before the 1967 Rose Bowl, the Purdue football team had some comfort level when facing USC.

The Trojans' coach was John McKay, who had played at Purdue in 1946 before transferring to Oregon. The Boilermakers also ran McKay's innovative I-formation offense that had been first installed by the Men of Troy in the early 1960s.

The coaches from the two schools, who were friends off the field and enjoyed the opportunity to socialize at team events leading up to the January 2 game, both agreed that the game was going to be like an intrasquad scrimmage.

The coaches were right. While many of the experts predicted a high-scoring affair, the Boilermakers and Trojans played a close-to-the-vest contest with few game-breaking plays. In the end, it came down to defense, which won it for Purdue. Defensive back George Catavolos intercepted a USC two-point conversion attempt with just over two minutes left in the game to secure a 14-13 Boilermaker victory.

Hawaiian Rescue

January 2, 1967, the date Purdue won the Rose Bowl over USC, is one of the most triumphant in the history of Purdue football. The date January 4, 1967, almost became one of the most tragic.

Just 48 hours after the Boilermakers' one-point win in Pasadena, two-time All-American quarterback Bob Griese and Rose Bowl hero George Catavolos nearly drowned off the beaches of Hawaii during a trip to the Hula Bowl.

According to a story told by Coach Jack Mollenkopf, Griese and Catavolos, who had saved the Boilermaker victory in Pasadena with an interception of a USC two-point conversion attempt, rented a Jeep to see the island. They stopped at an inviting beach on the North Shore of Oahu to do a little swimming, not realizing the strong undertow of the Pacific Ocean. At that time of year, the North Shore is home to some of the fiercest waves in the world and plays host to the international surfing championships.

Catavolos was the first to get into trouble, with Griese coming to his aid. Both swimmers grew tired trying to make it back to shore. Locals pulled them from the water.

Griese rebounded from the incident to toss three touchdown passes and kick a field goal and an extra point in the Hula Bowl three days later.

Griese and Catavolos's team, which was coached by Mollenkopf, pulled out a 28-27 win over the South squad that was headed by Florida quarterback Steve Spurrier, the player who nosed out Griese for the Heisman Trophy.

Leroy Legend

No single player in the history of Purdue captured the imagination of the college football world quite like Marvin Leroy Keyes. His on-the-field exploits are almost superhero-like.

Leroy ran. He kicked. He passed. He defended. He did it all.

As a sophomore in 1966, he played defensive back. But he still found time to toss two touchdown passes and run for a pair more. In fact, eight of the 12 halfback-option passes he completed during his college career went for touchdowns.

In his first big game at Notre Dame in 1966, he returned a Fighting Irish fumble 94 yards for a touchdown in the opening moments of the contest.

His junior year in 1967, Keyes moved over to the Boilermaker offense. All he did in his first season was lead the nation in scoring. But when things got tight in the pass defense department, Keyes returned to the Boilermaker secondary. He blanked stars such as Notre Dame's Jim Seymour like few had ever seen as he helped Purdue to a Big Ten title.

The following year, the nation knew of this gangly but graceful back from Newport News, Virginia, long before the season started. He graced the cover of *Sports Illustrated*, as Purdue was the preseason No. 1 team for the only time in school annals. While injuries curtailed what could have been a landmark season, Keyes still became the first player in school history to rush for 1,000 yards. In his last game, a miraculous 38-35 comeback win over Indiana, Keyes tied a school record with four touchdowns, including two in the final quarter.

Keyes, a two-time All-American, finished third in the race for the Heisman Trophy in 1967 and second in 1968. No Purdue player ever has finished in the top three two years running. He was tabbed Purdue's greatest football player ever in a fan vote in 1987.

The chant around Ross-Ade Stadium was "Give the Ball to Leroy." It was a magical time to be a Purdue fan, unlike any time before or since.

Sending Rick Home

It can be said that one of the great sales jobs in the history of Purdue basketball was the job head coach George King

Leroy Keyes

did to build his 1969 Final Four team.

Sure, it was a squad that had the great Rick Mount. But it also possessed a plethora of other notable talent.

For starters, King had a pair of seniors in Herman Gilliam and

Billy Keller who were legitimate Big Ten stars in their own right. The center, Chuck Bavis, was a highly recruited seven-footer who would be a scoring pivot man in most college programs. Getting these three talents to accept their roles made the Boilermakers a formidable force.

King, who had been an NBA star guard with Syracuse, winning the 1955 NBA crown, knew what it took to play in the pros. He flat-out guaranteed Gilliam that if he hung in there he would get his chance to be an NBA player. King was prophetic, as Gilliam enjoyed a decade-long professional career.

But the turning point in selling the trio to fulfill their respective roles came at practice early in Mount's career. King didn't like something Mount was doing and told him to "go on home."

King figured Mount would follow his command and head to the locker room. As it turned out, however, "The Rocket" really headed home. That is, about 40 miles south on U.S. Highway 52 to his boyhood home of Lebanon, Indiana. One of the basketball managers saw Mount packing his bags and alerted the coaching staff that Mount was heading out.

George King sent assistant Bob King, who had recruited Mount, down to Lebanon. Bob found Rick sitting at the dinner table at his mom's house and convinced his young star to come back to West Lafayette.

In this instance, the Boilermakers saw that George King was willing to discipline his star, even though Mount was one of the hardest workers on the team.

In the long run, it made the sales job to Gilliam, Keller and Bavis that much easier.

Leroy Thought he Could Ground the Rocket

L eroy Keyes could do anything on the football field. He ran, kicked, played in the secondary and passed in his days as a two-time All-American at Purdue.

Keyes also was a pretty fair basketball player. In the early days of Mackey Arena, the football team had its lockers in the new building. Late in the football season, Keyes and standout defensive end Billy McKoy often would find their way over to the Mackey Arena court to shoot a few jumpers before practice.

There were even a few times after the gridiron season concluded when the football players would play as a group against the basketball freshman before the varsity game. Keyes would tell the basketball coaching staff, "I can handle that Rick Mount guy, no problem."

Leroy and Mike: The Greatest Pass

It looked like Leroy Keyes's storybook career at Purdue was going to end on a down note. Much to the dismay of the capacity Ross-Ade Stadium crowd, archrival Indiana led Purdue 35-24 midway through the fourth quarter during the 1968 Old Oaken Bucket battle.

With Purdue facing second and 21 at its 44-yard line, the Hoosiers looked poised for the kill. Boilermaker quarterback Mike Phipps, who was nursing a tender ankle, was flushed out of the pocket and rolled toward the east sideline. Avoiding several Hoosier rushers and just a couple of steps from the boundary, Phipps planted off his wrong foot and heaved the ball toward the end zone. The Indiana defenders, figuring there was no way Phipps would get the pass off, let alone fling it with any accuracy, moved up.

There stood Keyes all alone at the IU two-yard line. He hauled in the Phipps pass and stepped into the end zone.

"It was the greatest pass I ever saw thrown in that stadium," said acting head coach Bob DeMoss, filling in for Jack Mollenkopf, who was battling hepatitis.

Phipps was on fire, and on the Boilermakers' next possession he completed five passes in a row. Keyes took it over from the two-yard line for his fourth touchdown of the game, and Purdue's dramatic 38-35 win over Indiana came to fruition.

George Was a Tough Guy

Ward "Piggy" Lambert, George King and Gene Keady had a lot in common. Not only are they the three greatest men's basketball coaches in school annals, but they had a reputation for refusing to back down in any situation.

King may have been the toughest of the bunch. Though he did not possess as demonstrative a bench demeanor as Lambert and Keady, he would pick and chose his moments to show stoutness. One of his most important duties was protecting his star Rick Mount against predatory defenses full of flying elbows and ferocious forearms. One cold February night in 1969 at Northwestern, Mount experienced especially rough treatment. After the Boilermakers' 13-point victory, Wildcats coach Larry Glass came to the Purdue locker room to congratulate Mount and Purdue on the win. Glass shook Mount's hand while King was in the restroom. King finished his business in time to pounce on Glass and pin him up against the locker room wall.

In front of several members of the team, King made it very clear to Glass that he did not appreciate his team's tactics.

"I'll never forget the look of intensity on George's face and the look of shock on Glass's," Mount said. "George's actions that night made us mentally tough."

Tough enough, that is, to go through the Big Ten schedule with a 13-1 record and advance to the NCAA championship game.

Rick Mount

Enough of Al's Tactics

Al McGuire became somewhat of a favorite of Boilermaker fans later in his life. As an analyst on NBC's national broadcasts in 1980 with Dick Enberg and Billy Packer, he nicknamed Joe Barry Carroll "The Aircraft Carrier." The moniker stuck with Carroll, not hurting his run at All-America honors. Eight years later, McGuire picked the Boilermakers as preseason No. 1, a team led by Troy Lewis, Todd Mitchell and Everette Stephens.

Purdue's first brush with McGuire, however, wasn't so pleasant. In the 1969 NCAA Mideast Regional Final game in Madison, Wisconsin, McGuire's Marquette Warriors (now called the Golden Eagles) faced the Boilermakers.

Purdue coach George King was well aware of McGuire's reputation of whipping his fans into a frenzy. Considering the Warriors were just 75 miles from home, King's concerns were valid. He had seen firsthand McGuire's theatrics two nights earlier when his team upset Adolph Rupp's Kentucky Wildcats with nearly 10,000 of the 13,025 fans in attendance on its side.

In an effort to keep McGuire at least a little bit under control, King asked an NCAA official before the game whether anything could be done about the Warriors' drum-beating band. The Boilermaker boss refused to allow McGuire to orchestrate things against his team like he had seen two nights before.

A trash talker long before it came in vogue, McGuire supposedly even went so far as to tell King before the game not to worry, because his Warriors were going to the Final Four. McGuire nearly was right, but the Boilermakers held on for a dramatic 75-73 overtime win.

McGuire would have to wait eight more years for his trip to the Final Four. He made the most of it, however, winning the national title after announcing his retirement from coaching.

The Screen and the Shot

O ne thing Rick Mount never lacked was confidence.
        In the 1969 NCAA Mideast Regional title game, Mount was having his worst shooting game of the season. Despite it, the Boilermakers still were in a position to pull out an improbable 75-73 overtime victory over Marquette in a game played in Madison, Wisconsin.

Purdue needed a miracle to get the game into the extra period. A heroic steal at midcourt by sophomore forward George

Faerber and subsequent missed free throws by Coach Al McGuire's Warriors gave Purdue the chance to break a 73-all tie. The teams went to the benches after a timeout was called with 26 seconds left in the extra period. Coach George King instructed his team to get the clock down to eight seconds and then have Mount, senior Herman Gilliam or super sophomore reserve Larry Weatherford take the game-winning shot.

Somehow Mount got the ball, and he wasn't going to let go of it. With eight ticks left he dribbled to the right corner. Reserve center Jerry Johnson, who had a career-high 16 rebounds in the game, had the presence of mind to set a solid screen on Marquette's Jack Burke. That gave Mount enough breathing room to get an edge on Burke, who had been hounding him all day. With his usual picture-perfect release, Mount let it fly with three seconds left. The ball softly went through the net, giving Purdue the two-point victory and its first trip to the Final Four.

Mount Makes it Level

The legend of Rick Mount, who starred on the hardwood for Purdue from 1968 to 1970, has many twists and turns. The story goes far beyond his 32.3 career scoring average that still stands as a Big Ten record. Not all of the things that added to Mount's lore occurred in game conditions.

Mount had the reputation of shooting a minimum of 500 jump shots a day since the age of five. He started with a tennis ball, shooting it into a tennis can, and worked his way up to a full-sized basketball and hoop.

All the while, Mount was developing one of the keenest shooting eyes in the history of college basketball. That vision was put to the test a few times in his college career. During his junior year in 1968-69, when the Boilermakers were making a run at their first Big Ten title in 29 years, "The Rocket" began to notice something wasn't quite right as the Boilermakers visited

Big Ten facilities.

On a trip to Bloomington, Mount was having trouble making his jumper during shooting practice. He turned to head coach George King and said, "That basket is not level." Considering that Mount had shot 2.25 million jump shots in his life at that point, King took Mount's claim seriously.

King, knowing he was in enemy territory and also knowing that the Hoosiers might do anything to slow down the Boilermakers, called the maintenance crew to check things out. Sure enough, it was determined that the basket was not level and was subsequently repaired.

The Boilermakers got out of Bloomington with a 96-95 win and 11 days later had a chance to clinch the title at Iowa. Once again in shooting practice, Mount called the maintenance crew out to check whether the basket was level. Once again it was askew, and the basket was replaced. Purdue beat the Hawkeyes 97-85.

By the time Purdue made its way to Louisville for the school's first-ever appearance in the Final Four, Mount's attention to detail was tested a third time. This time, however, the custodial staff at Freedom Hall was ready for it. In practice the day before the national semifinal game against North Carolina, and with a lot of media watching, Mount asked King to have the rim checked.

"I remember the custodian telling Coach King that Mount 'could put that rim where the sun doesn't shine,'" Mount said. "But in the end [when the rim was determined not to be level], he ended up apologizing to me. I wasn't trying to be difficult; I just knew something wasn't quite right."

The following night, things were just right for Mount and the Boilermakers. Purdue pounded Dean Smith's Tar Heels 92-65, thanks to 36 points from the deadly accurate Rocket.

Humbling Dean Smith

What is the closest thing to a flawless performance in Boilermaker men's basketball history?

It is probably the national semifinal of the 1969 NCAA Tournament. Sixth-ranked Purdue destroyed No. 4 North Carolina 92-65 to advance to the title game against UCLA.

To boot, college basketball's all-time winningest coach, Dean Smith, helped fuel the Boilermakers' fire before the two teams ever made it to Louisville's Freedom Hall for the contest. After Smith's Tar Heels slipped by Davidson by two points in the East Regional title game, he was quoted as saying he looked forward to a rematch of the 1968 title game with UCLA.

That did not sit too well with Purdue coach George King and the Boilermakers. Purdue proceeded to make easy work of North Carolina. Spurred by a gutsy move suggested by assistant coach Joe Sexson, the Boilermakers put their top scorer, Rick Mount, on North Carolina star Charlie Scott during a critical part of the game. Mount, not known for his defensive abilities, helped limit Scott to just 16 points. Mount also shot the lights out, scoring 36 points.

Senior guard Billy Keller had 20 points, but sustained a deep thigh bruise at the end of the game that cost the Boilermakers dearly in a loss to UCLA two days later.

After the game, Smith was gracious in defeat, calling Purdue "the best Big Ten team since Ohio State in the early 1960s. Nobody shoots like they do, and they are a better defensive team than we expected."

Lewis and Charles

Before he changed his name to Kareem Abdul-Jabbar, UCLA's Lew Alcindor terrorized the college basketball world, winning three national titles from 1967 to 1969. He was so dominant that after his sophomore season the NCAA disallowed dunking.

Keeping Alcindor under wraps was a relative thing, but no player in college basketball competed better against him than Boilermaker center Chuck Bavis. In the dedication game of Purdue Arena on December 2, 1967, Bavis and senior forward Roger Blalock helped slow Alcindor to just 17 points. Alcindor did manage 19 rebounds, including the all-important carom and outlet pass that led to a last-second game-winning basket by UCLA's Bill Sweek. In the rematch the following year in Los Angeles, Bavis contained Alcindor to just 18 points in the Bruins' 12-point victory.

When Purdue and UCLA later met for the 1969 national title, Bavis was on the pines after separating his shoulder in the first game of the NCAA Tournament against Miami (Ohio). Without Bavis in the game, Purdue was powerless to shut down Alcindor. The "big fella," as he was called at the time, scored 37 points and grabbed 20 rebounds to close out his collegiate career in style during a rousing 92-72 win.

After the game, UCLA head coach and three-time Boilermaker All-American John Wooden made his way over to the Purdue bench to talk to Bavis. In Wooden's typical formal and proper style he said to Bavis, "No one played Lewis tougher than you did, Charles. You should be very proud of that."

At the time, Bavis did not know he would never see the hardwood again. An automobile accident during the off season ended his career before his senior season.

Calling Off the Dogs, but Bitten Later

Purdue had just pulled off one of the greatest first halfs of football in its history. The Boilermakers were leading Woody Hayes's Ohio State Buckeyes 35-0 at halftime in

Columbus, Ohio, on October 14, 1967.

As the jubilant Boilermakers made their way into the locker room, no one could find head coach Jack Mollenkopf. After a minute or so, one of the Purdue assistant coaches located Mollenkopf, head in hands, sitting on a bench out of sight around the corner from the locker room.

An assistant came up to Mollenkopf and said, "What's wrong, Coach?"

Mollenkopf sat there quietly with a slight grin on his face and then muttered, "I must be dreaming."

A couple of Mollenkopf's lieutenants warned their boss that the locker room was filled with a bunch of guys who thought the game was over. Mollenkopf came to his senses and stomped into the locker room and delivered a gruff talk that got the team's attention.

The coach's short, but effective diatribe kept the wheels in motion when the Boilermakers took the field for the second half. The onslaught continued as the first-team offense, which included Mike Phipps, Leroy Keyes and Jim Beirne, scored in a handful of plays on its first possession to make the score 41-0. At that point, Mollenkopf gave the offense the rest of the day off. Ohio State managed to score on the last offensive drive of the game to avert a shutout.

At midfield after the game, Hayes thanked Mollenkopf for showing mercy on his team. Mollenkopf, an Ohio native, never had much use for Hayes, but accepted the gratitude. The next year, when the No. 1-ranked Boilermakers came calling in the 'Shoe, Hayes and his Buckeyes pitched a 13-0 shutout on their way to the 1968 national title.

The following year, Purdue made another trip back to Columbus and rainy and cold Ohio Stadium, with Phipps needing a big game to win the 1969 Heisman Trophy and the Boilermakers a huge upset to get to Pasadena. Ohio State had its way with Purdue, winning 42-14.

Despite the lopsided score, Hayes left his first team in the game well after the contest was decided. Mollenkopf was none too pleased at Hayes's short memory.

Pockets Picked in the Pocket City

When the defending Big Ten champion and NCAA runner-up Boilermaker basketball team made the trek to Evansville, Indiana, in December of 1969, it figured it might be in a for a little home cooking.

The Aces enticed Purdue to make the trip south by splitting the gate receipts. A good payday was in store because a capacity crowd of 12,000 was in attendance.

Purdue was without star guard Rick Mount, who had been sidelined for three weeks after suffering a knee strain against Butler. Evansville didn't feel sorry for the depleted visitors, as Coach Arad McCutcheon's team was thinking upset from the start. The Boilermakers looked like they might get out of town both with a win and the loot, but Evansville made a last-minute comeback to tie the score. With a couple seconds left, Evansville's John Wellemeyer, who scored a game-high 23 points, took one step and let the ball fly nearly 94 feet. The ball was just short of the rim and to the right.

Sophomore center William Franklin jumped and grabbed the ball as it neared the hoop. To the surprise of everyone, Richie Weiler, one of two Big Ten officials working the game, signaled goaltending in kind of a half-hearted style and promptly ran out of the gym. He wasn't going to get any complaints from the home fans, but Purdue coach George King was so mad after the contest that he vowed he would never bring another team to Evansville. He never did.

Fourteen years later, Gene Keady brought his fourth Boilermaker team to play in Evansville, and once again Purdue, who won the Big Ten later that season, went home with a loss. Like King had before him, Keady vowed that this would be his team's last trip to "The Pocket City."

To date, he has held true to his word.

"Big Cat" Eats "Big Dog" Alive

Purdue had a "Big Dog" on its men's basketball team before Glenn Robinson was even born. His name was William Franklin. One of the top five high school prospects in the nation in 1968, Franklin came to Purdue from Norfolk, Virginia, due to the notoriety of the Boilermaker basketball program, at the time buoyed by the legend of Rick Mount.

Franklin's self-proclaimed nickname lasted in the public eye about 24 hours. Purdue was playing in New York's Holiday Festival basketball tournament championship game on December 30, 1969. St. Bonaventure was the opponent and had its All-America center Bob "Big Cat" Lanier. The night before, after Purdue disposed of Pennsylvania to get to the title game, Franklin, in his first season of eligibility as a sophomore, made the mistake of telling the New York media that he was the "Big Dog" and was going to run the "Big Cat" out of Madison Square Garden. His picture was pasted in the Gotham newspapers the next morning and caused Coach George King to have trouble ingesting his coffee while perusing the morning papers.

All Lanier did was post a still-standing Purdue opponent record of 50 points to go with 15 rebounds. The undefeated and No. 12-ranked Bonnies blew out No. 17 Purdue 91-75. Lanier even played the game's final 33 minutes with a broken nose.

The Big Cat had eaten the Big Dog alive.

Uncle Knows Best

Defensive tackle Dave Butz was a two-time prep All-American in football from Maine South High School in Park Ridge, Illinois. In 1969, he had offers from 132 schools, including one from Coach Adolph Rupp at Kentucky, to play basketball.

In the end, however, Butz picked Purdue over Michigan after former Boilermaker head coach Jack Mollenkopf and assistant Ron Meyer recruited him.

In addition to Mollenkopf and Meyer, Purdue also got some help from one of its alumni.

Butz's uncle, Dr. Earl Butz, a Purdue graduate, was President Richard Nixon's Secretary of Agriculture. Butz received a phone call from his uncle, who was calling from the White House to put in a plug for his alma mater to his nephew.

"It was the one school which didn't offer any deals," Butz said. "They said, 'Come and participate in our athletic program and we'll make sure you'll get a good education.'"

Butz was part of a recruiting class that was one of Purdue's greatest ever. He joined the likes of Otis Armstrong, Darryl Stingley, Gary Danielson, Gregg Bingham and Steve Baumgartner, all of whom played in the NFL.

Butz is remembered as one of Purdue's most ferocious pass rushers and a catalyst on the Boilermaker "Doom Platoon" defense. At six foot seven, 315 pounds, wearing size 12, 7E (incredibly wide) shoes, Butz was as intimidating as they came.

When Butz was playing for the Boilermakers, former Michigan coach Bo Schembechler said, "That Butz is the best tackle I've seen … he's just magnificent."

Butz went on to have a tremendous NFL career with the St. Louis Cardinals (1973-75) and Washington Redskins (1976-88). He was a member of two Super Bowl championship teams (1982 and 1987). Butz, who bench-pressed 550 pounds, could leg-press 800, and ran a 5.0, 40-yard dash, finished his career with 560 solo tackles, 792 total, 16 1/2 forced fumbles, eight fumble recoveries and two interceptions.

His professional career nearly was short-lived. In the 1974 opener, he was hit below the left knee, which had to be surgically rebuilt. Butz overcame remarkable odds to return.

"I saw [the knee] fall off the X-ray table 90 degrees sideways," Butz said. "[The doctors] said I would never run again, but I fooled them."

In another example of his high pain threshold, he broke his thumb, sat out seven plays and returned to action. Another time he contracted intestinal parasites, was rushed to the hospital Saturday morning, and hours before kickoff Sunday had lost 33 pounds. After being pumped full of fluids, Butz went to the game, played and made a game-saving sack. He said the most painful moment came when he went back to the hospital and an intern, using a three-inch needle, couldn't find a vein in his arm.

Butz says his Purdue roots held into his professional career. Virtually all knew he was a former Boilermaker, even veteran broadcaster Howard Cosell, who, in his trademark voice, said upon seeing Butz after a game in Washington, "Dave Butz out of Purdue."

"I thought, damn, he even talks like that in person," Butz said.

Never Let 'Em See You Sweat

Len Dawson and Hank Stram began their long relationship at Purdue when Stram was an assistant under Coach Stu Holcomb and Dawson enrolled at Purdue to play quarterback in 1953. They always seemed to understand one another.

Dawson was a very particular and precise sort, even in the way he spoke. Stram was a flashy dresser, but possessed a much more laid-back personality.

One time when Stram was coaching Dawson and the Kansas Chiefs against the archrival Oakland Raiders, Dawson came over to the bench after being thumped to the ground by the vicious Raiders' rush.

"Who was supposed to block that fellow on that play?" Dawson calmly asked his coach. Stram replied, "Leonard [as Stram referred to his prized quarterback almost to match Dawson's formal nature], don't worry about who was supposed to block on that play. I am more worried about the Raiders seeing you sweat."

"Coach," Dawson said as if to interrupt his coach, "quarterbacks don't sweat ... they perspire."

Basketball is a Contact Sport

Three of Purdue's greatest quarterbacks also played on the Purdue basketball team early in their careers.

Bob DeMoss was a member of the freshman team in 1945-46. Len Dawson played as a freshman and then made the team as a junior before quitting near Christmas of the 1955-56 season. Bob Griese was a part-time starter on the varsity through his sophomore season. He gave up basketball, not because he wanted to, but because his football coach, Jack Mollenkopf, happened to pop in on basketball practice at the wrong time.

Griese showed a lot of promise on the gridiron, leading the Boilermakers to a 6-3 record in 1964. After the season concluded with a win over Indiana, the Evansville, Indiana, native joined Ray Eddy's basketball team as a playmaking guard. Though not a big offensive threat on the hardwood, he possessed the great leadership skills that resulted in winning, as he did on the gridiron.

Mollenkopf had at best a passing interest in basketball, but with his franchise player battling it out on the hardwood, his trips to the fieldhouse to observe practice became more frequent. One time after watching Griese battle for a loose ball during a workout, Mollenkopf pulled one of the assistant coaches over to the side and stated the obvious.

"Basketball is kind of rough, isn't it?" Mollenkopf said rhetorically. "Somebody could get hurt out there."

Griese's basketball career pretty much ended at that point.

Mollenkopf wasn't against looking at Purdue's basketball talent for football. One player who caught Mollenkopf's eye was a solidly built freshman named George Faerber in the fall of 1967.

In the early days of the brand-new Purdue Arena, both the football and basketball teams shared locker space on the east side of the lower level. Mollenkopf came up to Faerber after practice one day, saying, "I heard you played some football in high school; what position?"

"Linebacker, sir," Faerber said.

"Your legs are too fat to play basketball," Mollenkopf said. "You should be playing football."

Faerber's "fat" legs carried him to three years as a starting forward, playing a key role in the Boilermakers' a 59-18 record first trip to the Final Four. Mollenkopf, meanwhile, never asked Faerber again about playing football.

Lamar Was Fearsome

L amar Lundy was a man the second he set foot on the football field for Purdue. As a sophomore in 1954, he split time at offensive and defensive end. Standing six foot seven, he was an imposing physical presence for that time period.

It didn't take Lundy long to make his mark at Purdue. In his second college game, he caught a long touchdown pass from Len Dawson to break open the contest in the Boilermakers' 27-14 upset of the No. 1 Fighting Irish.

The following week, Duke, ranked sixth in the country, thought they would take advantage of the youthful Lundy. Early in the game, future NFL Hall of Fame quarterback Sonny Jurgenson called three running plays right at Lundy. Three plays later, it was fourth and 12 for the Blue Devils.

Word must have traveled fast to the Boilermaker opposition, because it was the last time in his college career that any offense tried to challenge Lundy one on one. In the 1960s, Lundy proved worthy of the attention, or lack of it, as he became a member of the Los Angeles Rams' "Fearsome Foursome," the most revered pass-rushing unit in the history of the game.

Purdue's Yogi Berra

S am Voinoff was proud of his Bulgarian heritage. But sometimes he struggled to fully understand English phrases.

Rugged enough to stand tall in the gridiron trenches as a 165-pound guard on Purdue's undisputed 1929 Big Ten title team, Voinoff also served 14 years as an assistant football coach under Mal Elward, Cecil Isbell and Stu Holcomb. His legendary phrase "pair 'em up in threes" still resonates among some longtime followers of Purdue.

Voinoff's success as Purdue's golf coach during his 25-year stint is unprecedented in school history. His teams won 10 Big Ten titles and one NCAA team championship. In addition, he coached Joe Campbell to the 1955 NCAA individual championship that was determined by match play. He also mentored six individual conference champions and five All-Americans. All of this occurred despite Voinoff possessing a golf game that was more of a work in progress than a piece of art.

One of his shining moments came after the Boilermakers' third consecutive Big Ten crown in 1960. Ohio State coach Bob Kepler, a legendary coach in his own right, approached Voinoff half in admiration and half in frustration. After hearing Kepler utter a few words, Voinoff assumed Kepler was mad at him. When Voinoff got flustered, his eastern European English came to the forefront, and his phrases often were entertaining but made little sense.

"How do you keep winning?" asked Kepler, who had a sophomore named Jack Nicklaus on the 1960 squad. "We have some of the best players and you always find a way to beat us."

Voinoff didn't know what to say and began his response in almost an apologetic mode.

"I don't know how we keep winning," he responded. "I guess it is because we have players who are from out of the country like New York and Pennsylvania."

Kepler had his answer and Voinoff had his championship.

CHAPTER 4

1970s

The Paper Airplane Game

What is the wildest game in Mackey Arena history? To this day, it remains the Iowa game on February 28, 1970.

Rick Mount shattered the Big Ten scoring record with 61 points in the most amazing flurry of offense ever seen in conference play. The Boilermakers never had been beaten in a conference game in nearly three years in their new arena and were riding a 30-game home victory streak.

Mount scored 32 points in the first half against No. 8 Iowa. He ran his total to 45 points with 13 minutes left in the game and Purdue clinging to a three-point lead. That's when things really got strange.

Following successive foul calls on Boilermaker guard Steve Longfellow, a paper airplane sailed out of the south stands. The raucous Purdue crowd had been warned earlier by referee Bob Brodbeck, via a public address announcement, for throwing debris on the court.

Brodbeck made good on his warning, and for the only time in Purdue basketball history, a technical foul was whistled against the crowd. A fiery Coach George King refused to talk to Brodbeck as he came over to explain the call. King went to the length of the railing to go into the stands as a sign of his disgust.

Longtime Purdue fans contend the airplane came from the Iowa cheering section. But the Hawkeyes had received only two dozen tickets to the game, and most were directly behind the Iowa bench. When the smoke cleared on the incredible sequence, the visitors had a six-point play and a 70-67 lead.

Ultimately, Purdue let a nine-point lead with just over two minutes to go slip away, as Iowa guard Fred "Downtown" Brown caught fire to lead the Hawks to a 108-107 win and a Big Ten title.

Mount's performance would have been even more incredible had there been a three-point shot. Thirteen of his 27 field goals were from behind the arc. By today's standards "The Rocket" would have enjoyed a cool 74 points for the afternoon.

No one has come close to breaking Mount's 61-point mark since in Big Ten play. Had the three-point play been in effect, Mount's 74-point effort might have entered the "record never to be broken" category.

Fateful First Meeting

Eight years before former Purdue receiver Darryl Stingley sustained the hit from Jack Tatum that would put him permanently in a wheelchair, the two had a violent collision in Ross-Ade Stadium.

On an inclement day in West Lafayette on November 14, 1970, third-ranked Ohio State was a heavy favorite over Purdue. The Boilermakers, struggling under first-year coach Bob DeMoss with a 3-5 record, played the Buckeyes tough before falling 10-7. Looking back, however, Stingley remembered little more about that game than the eerie first encounter with Tatum.

As a gangly sophomore, Stingley was knocked unconscious twice in the contest, once on the sideline on a blow delivered by Tatum.

"I met up with my nemesis, Jack Tatum, who would eventually change my life forever," said Stingley of his first encounter with the Ohio State defensive back. "[After being hit,] I nearly went into convulsions from swallowing my tongue.

"Little did I know that I would encounter him again many years later as a professional and he would have the [same] type of attitude. He thought he had to make an impression on his coaches with violent hits."

Stingley still has not spoken with Tatum a quarter-century after his paralyzing injury.

A Call From the President

Purdue had just left their collective hearts on the field in a 10-7 loss to Ohio State in front of a national television audience in November 1970.

On a day of nasty weather in Ross-Ade Stadium, the Boilermakers had trouble moving the ball in rain and sleet. In the closing minutes, Purdue drove inside the Buckeye 10-yard line and decided to go for the win instead of the tie on fourth and one. Rookie head coach Bob DeMoss had used the diminutive Stanley Brown as a human airplane to sail over the line with great success in short-yardage situations.

But for the first and only time in Brown's career, the Buckeyes grounded the Boilermaker aerial offensive and stopped Purdue to seal the win.

In those days, there weren't many college football games on television, but this game was nationally broadcast on ABC. It so happened that President Richard Nixon was watching the game. Nixon was so impressed by the Boilermakers' willingness to go for it all and the great college football game that he called both teams' locker rooms after the contest.

After addressing his downtrodden team, DeMoss was told he had a phone call from the President. Fully expecting it to be university president Frederick Hovde, DeMoss was quite surprised to hear Nixon on the other end of the line.

Nixon reportedly guaranteed Purdue that it would be in the Rose Bowl before DeMoss's talented collection of sophomores completed their eligibility. It was a reasonable statement considering that group included Otis Armstrong, Dave Butz, Gary Danielson and Darryl Stingley.

Much like the Nixon presidency, however, the Boilermakers fell short of reaching their desired destination.

Winning from the Wheelchair

G eorge King was a great basketball player in his own right. His backcourt play helped take Syracuse to the 1955 NBA crown.

In addition to the world title, King took a bum knee away from his professional basketball career. Fifteen years later, while serving as the Boilermakers' head basketball coach, King's knee condition was bad enough that he had to have surgery during the middle of the season.

During the medical process, King missed a game and joined the team in Lexington, Kentucky, for the 1970 Kentucky Invitational (UKIT). After the Boilermakers defeated defending Big Eight champion Kansas State in the first round, they faced third-ranked Kentucky and its legendary coach, Adolph Rupp, in the title game.

Watching in near disbelief from a wheelchair, King saw his team dismantle the No. 3 Wildcats in the second half. It was the first time someone other than Rupp's team had won the UKIT since 1964 and snapped a 25-game Wildcats home winning streak. Larry Weatherford, a talented guard from Evansville, Indiana, was named the tournament Most Valuable Player after scoring 57 points in the two games. The surprising victory in Bluegrass Country no doubt helped King in the recovery process.

A month later, however, the Boilermakers' play had the opposite effect on their coach. King grew frustrated with his team after a nonresponsive first half against Marshall. Out of his wheelchair and for a moment forgetting he had recently had knee surgery, King kicked a container just prior to addressing his players at halftime. He mistakenly thought it was empty but quickly found out it was full of wet towels.

Purdue pulled out the victory over the Thundering Herd, but King spent the rest of the game in severe pain after reinjuring the knee he had worked so hard to mend.

Morgan Sold Mums

There is little telling what life events will have an impact on an individual's future. For a swimmer from Munster, Indiana, named Morgan Burke, one of his experiences in college shaped his management style as Purdue's 11th athletics director.

As a collegian, Burke competed on the Purdue swimming team. He captained the squad his senior year of 1972-73. While Burke loved his athletics experience at Purdue, he remembered having to pedal mums and game programs at Purdue football games just to raise money for team trips and expenses. In those days, there was little money for sports besides football and basketball.

When Burke took the job as head of the athletics department on January 1, 1993, he vowed to himself that he would raise the bar for all sports on all fronts—academic, athletic and financial support. Of Burke's greatest accomplishments in his first decade at Purdue, what he has done to raise funding and improve facilities for all sports is high on the list.

Larry and the Three Renegades

Purdue's 1972 4x100-meter relay team had about as little talent as one could have and still come within an eyelash of winning a national championship. Sure, it didn't hurt to have the speed of Olympian Larry Burton to anchor the relay, but Carl Capria, Larry Grambo and Dave Lichtenheld proved to be a magic unit.

Capria was a defensive back on the football team who later played in the NFL for the Detroit Lions. Grambo was from Gary, Indiana, and came to Purdue thanks in part to George Steinbrenner. Grambo's father was involved with the unions in Lake County, and Steinbrenner's American Shipbuilding Company was having some labor relations problems in that area at the time. Steinbrenner called Purdue to ask the school to recruit Grambo as a favor to Grambo's father. Of course, it also helped Steinbrenner get out of a labor pickle. Steinbrenner reportedly also threw a little money Purdue's way to help pay for the scholarship. Lichtenheld was the glue of the unit. Coach Dave Rankin instructed him to pull the relay team together.

After the race, which was televised nationally on ABC's *Wide World of Sports,* Steinbrenner called Rankin to say, "You must be the greatest coach in America to make All-Americans on a relay team with one great runner."

That great runner, Burton, won the 200 meters at the same meet and finished fourth in the 1972 Olympics in Munich, Germany. Burton joined Orval Martin (1930, 880-yard run), Duane Purvis (1933, javelin) and Jim Johnson (1958, pole vault) as the only Boilermakers to win national titles in outdoor track and field.

Duane Purvis

Pinky Saw Red

William "Pinky" Newell was a pioneer in athletic
training, serving as head athletic trainer from 1949 to
1978. He helped found the National Athletic Trainers Association
and was the NATA's executive secretary from 1955 to 1967. But
as much as anything, Newell, who played football for Purdue in

the 1940s, hated Indiana University.

Newell had just hired a new assistant trainer named Denny Miller in the fall of 1973. When the Boilermakers were set to face Indiana in the season finale in Bloomington, Miller saw a side of his boss he could barely believe.

Moments after the Boilermakers scored a touchdown early in the game, Miller found himself face down on the Memorial Stadium turf like he had been run over from behind.

When he pulled himself off the turf, he quickly realized it was Newell who had played steamroller. He turned to look at his red-faced boss, who was shaking and screaming at him.

"Now G— damn it, that is the way it is supposed to be!" Newell screamed, almost in full convulsion. From that moment forward, Miller, who has spent the last 30 years of an illustrious career as Purdue's head athletic trainer, knew the battle for the Old Oaken Bucket was more than a football game.

Sweet Smell of Success in the Garden

Fred Schaus came to Purdue in the spring of 1972 to replace his good friend George King as the Boilermakers' head basketball coach. Schaus had been the general manager of the Los Angeles Lakers when they won the 1972 NBA crown, but he had grown weary of the pro game and the Los Angeles lifestyle.

King, who served under Schaus as an assistant coach at West Virginia, convinced his former boss that the idyllic campus life would suit him and his family much better than the City of Angels. So Schaus came to Purdue and even bought a pickup truck and some farmland in the Lafayette area to get into the Hoosier mood.

Schaus loved the fast-break style that had been a Boilermaker mainstay under all coaches since the days of Piggy Lambert. And Schaus had early success. It took him just two years to make a big impact.

The NCAA Tournament was composed of just 32 teams at the time. Purdue, which fell just short of Michigan and Indiana in the 1974 conference race, became the first Big Ten team to win the National Invitation Tournament at New York's Madison Square Garden.

In those days, all the games in the NIT were played at The Garden. Purdue upset No. 8 North Carolina in the first round, gained sweet redemption for a regular-season loss to Hawaii in round two, easily handled Jacksonville in the semifinals and then turned the tables for a bitter loss earlier in the year by defeating Utah.

The Boilermakers were blessed with some special senior leaders in Frank Kendrick, David Luke and Bruce Rose. Schaus's style relied on his seniors to provide much of the leadership and a set a good example with respect to team discipline. Kendrick, Luke and Rose each proved very capable in that area.

The Boilermakers had a perfect blend of players that year. With Purdue's all-time assist leader in Bruce Parkinson running the offense, super-defender Jerry Nichols, who blew out his knee in the quarterfinal game against Hawaii, and talented big man John Garrett, who was a big-time scorer, the Boilermakers ended up the season ranked 11th nationally. That team will be remembered as one of the better ones in school annals.

Alex's Giant Slayers

A lex Agase's tenure as the Boilermakers' head football coach from 1973 to 1976 did not go as planned. When he was hired to replace Bob DeMoss after the 1972 season, athletics director George King and many others close to the football program figured Agase was a perfect fit for the job.

After all, he was an All-America guard on Purdue's undefeated 1943 team and had enjoyed a reasonable amount of coaching success from 1964 to 1972 at one of the toughest schools at which to gather victories, Northwestern. His record wasn't flashy after succeeding Ara Parseghian in Evanston, but he had the Wildcats competitive most years and downright dangerous in 1970 and 1971, when they were in the hunt for the conference title.

Initially, Agase was a popular choice with Purdue fans. He had a reputation of being a good recruiter who had been successful in landing talent in the Chicago area—historically a spot of focus for cultivating future Boilermakers.

Much like Jack Mollenkopf, Agase was not a flashy dresser or someone who impressed you with his style. He was a no-nonsense guy whom the media enjoyed and fans, once they got to know him, liked as well.

The problem with Agase's tenure at Purdue, however, was that he did not win enough for the fans to get to know him. But to his credit, Agase was able to get his team to rise to the occasion for two of the most memorable wins in school history.

In 1974, the Boilermakers were a 35-point underdog at defending national champion Notre Dame. Purdue played maybe the greatest quarter in its history by jumping to a 24-0 lead in the first quarter under the shadow of the golden dome. Agase's boys held on for dear life as the Boilermakers won 31-20. It was Parseghian's last game against Purdue.

Two years later, Purdue was more than a three-touchdown underdog against No. 1 Michigan in Ross-Ade Stadium. Quite frankly, no one gave Purdue a chance. The Boilermakers had been embarrassed the week before in a 45-13 loss at Michigan State and were banged up. Coach Bo Schembechler's Wolverines appeared ready to name the score as they marched down the field on their first possession for a quick 7-0 lead. It took an incredible performance by the Boilermakers' defense and a courageous effort by back Scott Dierking. Nursing a swollen ankle, Dierking rushed for 162 yards on 38 carries and did much to keep Michigan's ball-controlled offense off the field. It was enough to pull off a 16-14 triumph and spoil Schembechler's best chance at a national title—something he never earned during his fabled career at Michigan.

In the end, however, attendance was dwindling, and when Agase's team could not beat Indiana in the season finale two weeks after the Michigan triumph, King was forced to let Agase go.

Finding a
Rocky Mountain High

During his eight years as an assistant basketball coach, George Faerber saw many parts of the United States. He also received many calls from scouts and well-intentioned alumni wanting him to go see a particular player or players.

When he received a call from Denver from a Purdue fan in December of 1975, he thought little of it. Colorado wasn't a hot spot for college talent and not an region of emphasis for the school's recruiting effort.

The Purdue fan said there were two players Purdue should see—a 6'8" forward and a 6'2" guard. Faerber told the fan that he would check the scouting reports and get back with him.

The supporter persisted, and Faerber finally decided he would make the trip to the Denver area during the team's road swing through Iowa. After seeing the 6'8" player the first night, Faerber was impressed not only with the player's talent, but with the eye for talent his newfound friend possessed. The player turned out to be Tom Chambers, who enjoyed an all-star NBA career. The Boilermakers tried unsuccessfully to lure him away from the University of Utah.

The next night, Faerber went to see the 6'2" player. His friend said there was also a seven-footer that he was not too impressed with, but that Faerber would really love the guard.

"When I saw the seven-footer in warmups, that was all I needed to see," Faerber said. "My host kept apologizing about the big guy, but as it turned out, he was the one worth seeing."

About 30 days later, Purdue won a hard-fought recruiting battle for the services of the gangly center named Joe Barry Carroll out of East High School. Missouri had been on Carroll for three years and Kentucky got into the recruiting game late, but Purdue's more laid-back atmosphere turned out to be the biggest attraction for the reticent Carroll.

Faerber's diamond in the rough became the school's all-time leading rebounder and No. 2 scorer.

Joe Barry Carroll

Getting a Glimpse of Magic

During a Boilermaker road trip to Michigan State in February of 1976, assistant coach George Faerber asked head coach Fred Schaus if he wanted to join him on a short trip to see a high school player that evening.

Schaus passed on Faerber's offer, but when Faerber returned, the Boilermaker mentor asked, "Well, what did you think?"

"College or pro?" Faerber said.

"What do you mean, college or pro?" Schaus said.

"This guy is so good as a high school junior that he could play for any pro team out there," Faerber retorted. "He is that good."

"Ah, no way, you must be kidding," said Schaus, who had spent three decades as a player and coach in the professional game. "There is no way a high school junior could be that good."

Who was that high school junior? Earvin "Magic" Johnson.

"I never saw a better player at that age in all of my years of watching basketball," Faerber said years later.

A Dapper Dandy

After Fred Schaus recruited Kyle Macy to play basketball for Purdue in early April of 1975, the Boilermakers had the good fortune of possessing one of the best trio of guards in the nation. Macy was a first-team high school All-American from Peru, Indiana, and the Boilermakers already had starters Eugene Parker and Bruce Parkinson returning.

Therefore, the Purdue coaching staff held little hope of getting another standout guard from Martinsville, Indiana, named Jerry Sichting. At the time, there had been a lot of jockeying for recruiting position going on between Indiana and Purdue for Sichting, Macy and another top guard from Illinois named Bob Bender.

Though Bender would later commit to Indiana, he had not done so by the time of The Dapper Dan Classic to be played in

Louisville's Freedom Hall. Sichting was getting a lot of pressure from Louisville's Denny Crum to commit, but he also was very interested in playing 15 miles down the road at IU.

Faerber, who was in the Bluegrass State for the game, knew that Sichting was a uniquely competitive kid. When he saw him after the contest he asked Sichting an important question.

"Since Kyle committed to Purdue I'll bet you have been getting a few phone calls from other schools saying Purdue is out of the picture for you," Faerber told Sichting. "How does that make you feel?"

"To be honest, I think people are trying to tell me that since Macy is going to Purdue, I am not going to be able to play [there]," Sichting said.

"Do you have any doubt you can play at Purdue and that you will get court time?" Faerber shot back.

"I have no doubt," Sichting said.

As matters played out, the fact Purdue had recruited Macy turned out to be a positive in the recruitment of Sichting.

In the end, things worked out pretty well for Sichting at Purdue. Macy left the Boilermakers for Kentucky after his freshman season, and Bender left IU for Duke a year later. Sichting, meanwhile, directed Purdue to a Big Ten title his senior year in 1979 and played on an NBA championship team in Boston in 1986. Macy's pro career fizzled.

Kyle to Kentucky

Peru, Indiana, a small town in the north central part of the state, produced two of the top high school players in the country in the early 1970s. John Garrett, a six-foot-11 center with a great shooting touch, was a three-year standout for the Boilermakers from 1973 to 1975. Kyle Macy, a smooth-shooting guard, was a 1975 *Parade* All-American before choosing to attend Purdue.

The recruiting battle was keen for both players. Purdue had help securing the talented duo from the Peru townspeople, especially from area business owner and Purdue alum Barry Touloukian.

In those days, it was within NCAA rules for alumni to get involved with the recruiting process. Touloukian became the eyes and ears for the Boilermaker coaching staff, reporting Garrett and Macy's every move. When North Carolina or Duke would come in for a visit, the results of the meeting quickly were relayed to the Purdue brass. It proved beneficial in landing the two stars.

Not surprisingly, Macy came to Purdue under a lot of fanfare. The Boilermakers had signed one of the best backcourts in a single recruiting year in the history of the program when Martinsville, Indiana, star Jerry Sichting decided to join Macy at Purdue.

Macy's days at Purdue, however, were short. Thanks to a wrist injury to starting senior guard Bruce Parkinson in the second game of the 1975-76 season, Macy started 25 games as a freshman, averaging an impressive 13.8 points per contest. But after the season was over, Macy gave Coach Fred Schaus news the Boilermaker boss never recovered from.

Macy was transferring to Kentucky.

Parkinson decided to return for a fifth year, giving up a high NBA draft choice, and was blamed by many fans for Macy's departure. The real story, however, was that Macy's father, who also served as his high school coach, was unhappy with some of the remaining players' attitudes toward his son. To no one's surprise, Macy ended up at Kentucky and helped the Wildcats win the 1978 NCAA title.

Schaus's 1976-77 team became the second Boilermaker squad to be selected to the NCAA Tournament, but the 1977-78 squad, still possessing some of the same team chemistry issues, grossly underachieved. At the end of the year, Schaus decided he had had enough of college basketball coaching.

Cleveland Pittsburgh Excuses Himself

When Jim Young was hired to lead the Purdue football program prior to the 1977 season, one of the most talented returning players left over from Alex Agase's regime was a defensive tackle named Cleveland Crosby.

Actually, his name was Cleveland Pittsburgh Crosby.

Crosby was big and talented, but he didn't like to practice too much. He used to fake heart trouble during running drills. As with any new coach, Young had to get the attention of his team and impress upon the unit that hard work was the only answer to turning the program back into a winner.

Predictably, Crosby did not take a liking to Young's conditioning drills. One day after a strenuous workout, Crosby quit the team.

The following day, however, Crosby came back to the coaches and said he had made a big mistake. Young told Crosby that he would ask the team if it wanted Crosby back at a squad meeting later that day.

At the team meeting, the Boilermaker unit agreed to take Crosby back. Young, trying to build unity and responsibility on his squad, accepted the team's decision.

Crosby didn't last long, however. Young had the squad return to the ghastly drills. Crosby ran one lap of the 12-minute run and just kept on running and never came back.

Ironically, Crosby finished his college career at Arizona, where Young had coached before coming to Purdue. The fact that Young would run off the star player sent a clear message to the rest of the team.

Twenty years later, history would repeat itself in the Purdue football program. First-year coach Joe Tiller dismissed his top returning linebacker, Chike Okeafor, from the team for a year. Okeafor did return the following year after meeting Tiller's stringent guidelines. Tiller's temporary dismissal of Okeafor equally sent a distinct message to the team.

It is not surprising that Tiller and Young are two of the most successful coaches in the history of Purdue football.

Carmel Connection Nearly Disconnected

One of the most famous passing combinations nearly didn't come to pass at Purdue.

Mark Herrmann and Bart Burrell grew up in Carmel, Indiana, and have been friends since grade school. They played on a state high school championship football team for the Greyhounds as juniors and then were on the same front line of Carmel's state champion boys' basketball team a year later.

Herrmann was highly recruited out of high school. Had Purdue not changed coaches from the run-oriented style of Alex Agase to the pass-oriented attack of Jim Young, Herrmann likely would have picked another school.

Burrell, on the other hand, had no Division I scholarship offers. Near his hometown, Butler had expressed interest but was offering less than a full scholarship. Burrell wanted to prove he could play at the college level and decided he would be a Bulldog.

At the Indiana All-Star football game at the Butler Bowl in Indianapolis, Young happened to be in the stands watching his prized quarterback. It was there he noticed Burrell on the receiving end of several of Herrmann's passes. Young also laid eyes on a defensive end wearing jersey No. 66 named John Macon, who happened to run the ball a few times as a fullback. Macon was headed for the University of Evansville.

Young, who happened to be sitting at the game with the Butler and Evansville coaches, quietly asked his coaching colleagues about Macon and Burrell. He got an answer, though he really didn't need one. Young surmised that the two could play in the Big Ten.

Due to a couple of academic casualties, Purdue just happened to have a couple of available scholarships. Young signed Macon

Mark Herrmann

and Burrell a few days later.

Burrell was hell bent on proving he belonged in the Big Ten and not settling on just being happy to be on the team. He did that with an exclamation point, graduating from Purdue third on its all-time list with 140 receptions.

Macon had a standout career, as well, leading the Boilermakers in rushing in 1978 and ranking sixth on the all-time rushing list when his playing days concluded in 1980.

The Hit that Helped Make Montana Famous

Purdue had Notre Dame on the ropes on September 24, 1977.

Boilermaker linebacker and team Most Valuable Player Fred Arrington delivered one of the most vicious legal blows ever seen in Ross-Ade Stadium. The hit rendered second-string Fighting Irish quarterback Gary Forystek, who had been effective in his brief appearance, nearly lifeless on the turf in the first quarter. Rusty Lisch, who started the game, returned to the contest. He tossed two touchdown passes in the second quarter, but couldn't lead the Irish to a score in the first three possessions after halftime.

Had Forystek not been injured, he probably never would have left the game. Instead, after Lisch was ineffective, Irish coach Dan Devine turned to third-string quarterback Joe Montana for the game's final 15 minutes.

Freshman quarterback Mark Herrmann had passed the Irish silly in the first half with 254 yards through the air. Notre Dame had slowed Herrmann down in the third quarter, but the Boilermakers still were in control of the game, leading 24-14.

Montana, who had sat out the 1976 season due to a shoulder injury, settled down after having his first pass in a college game in nearly two years nearly intercepted. He didn't throw deep, but he methodically picked apart the Purdue secondary, completing nine of 14 fourth-quarter passes for 154 yards and a touchdown. The Irish's 17 fourth-quarter points were enough to rally Notre Dame to a 31-24 win.

Montana led the Irish to 11 straight wins and the 1977 national title. He later won four Super Bowl titles with the San Francisco 49ers. But his legend of orchestrating great comebacks and big victories started against Purdue. And in a bizarre twist of fate, he has Arrington to thank for finally getting his chance.

Quiet Ride Home

One of the worst sports tragedies of all time involved the University of Evansville basketball team. On a rainy, foggy night on December 13, 1977, members of the Aces and university personnel were among the 29 people killed when their airplane crashed shortly after takeoff from the Evansville airport.

Also among the dead was Greg Knipping, who had served as the Purdue sports information director just a year earlier.

In a tragic case of irony, the same plane had delivered Purdue to Louisville the night before for a game with Denny Crum's Cardinals. Following a heart-wrenching 68-66 loss at Freedom Hall, the ill-fated aircraft was to take Purdue back to West Lafayette.

When word came to the Purdue travel party of the tragedy, the Boilermakers boarded a bus for the three-hour trip home.

It was a quiet bus ride.

Rose Liked 'Em
Six Foot Five or Better

Lee Rose was a master at mind games. He wasted little time getting into the heads of his backcourt after he took the men's basketball job at Purdue in April of 1978. It happened in one of his first team meetings.

Rose came to Purdue after taking Charlotte to the Final Four in 1977. Silver-haired in his early 40s, Rose had a stately look about him for a man who was not physically assuming.

At the early team meeting, Rose outlined his expectations for his team. He went through many of the usual things like teamwork, mutual respect and his penchant for controlling the game's tempo. Toward the end of the meeting, however, he made the seemingly offhand comment that he liked his guards six foot five or better.

Returning starter Jerry Sichting, who barely stood 6'1", and transfer Brian Walker, who was 6'2", looked at one another as if they had seen a ghost.

Though Rose had received a commitment from 6'5" guard Keith Edmonson, Rose knew all along that Walker and Sichting were going to be his guards. He also knew of the competitive nature of the pair and that his comments would light a fire under them.

Rose had his faults as a coach, but there was no one better at pushing the buttons of certain players (especially the starters) to make them perform. The Boilermakers won a share of the Big Ten title and finished runner-up in the NIT in 1979 with Walker and Sichting running the show.

Scooby Would Have Driven

Michael "Scooby-Doo" Scearce was one of the most likeable, yet naïve, freshman members of the men's basketball team in the fall of 1978. With a body that resembled the cartoon character, Scearce was looking forward to the team's trip to Hawaii to play in the Rainbow Classic over the holidays.

At the conclusion of practice before the team left on the trip, first-year coach Lee Rose gathered the team at center court of Mackey Arena to give some final instructions. Rose, ever the planner, instructed his team to get lots of rest because it was going to be a long flight to Honolulu the following day. How long Rose wasn't certain, but it would be a long day.

Scearce might have been a rookie, but he never was afraid to speak up. So before the huddle dispersed, Scooby piped in with a thought-provoking question.

"How long would it take us to drive?" Scearce said.

Herm Always Kept His Cool

Coach Jim Young, who led the Boilermaker football program from 1977 to 1981, always was way ahead of his time. An example of his forward thinking was he hired a sports psychologist nearly a decade before it became fashionable to do so.

The sports psychologist followed the team around. He also spent time with individuals in hopes of molding the Boilermakers into a more cohesive unit.

One time, in front of the whole team, the sports shrink wanted to show how much the heart rate increases when a player is under stress. He summoned sophomore quarterback Mark Herrmann to the front of the lecture room and attached monitors to the star's chest.

"You'll see Mark's heart rate increase as we show game film and increase the volume on the crowd noise," the doctor told the Boilermakers.

With Herrmann wired, he rolled out game film of Herrmann sustaining hits from rushing lineman and running for his life under tenacious pursuit.

The result: There was no increase in Herrmann's heart rate.

Then the psychologist brought in a blaring radio broadcast full of crowd noise that corresponded to more game film of Herrmann running for his life.

Still no increase.

Nothing the sports psychologist did that day could raise Herrmann's anxiety level or his heart rate. The test confirmed what the football team already knew. There was a calm, cool dude behind center.

Not even establishing an NCAA record for career passing yardage in his senior year against Michigan State could raise Herrmann's blood pressure or excitement level.

The same could not be said for opposing coaches.

No More Stick-um

It was back in the days of Lester Hayes and Fred Biletnikoff. The two Oakland Raiders stars were famous for applying lots of stick-um on their hands to help them catch the football during the mid- to late 1970s. Hayes did it in the secondary and Biletnikoff as a wide receiver.

The trend made its way to college football a couple years later and even found its way to the Purdue football team. During a nip-and-tuck game at Iowa in 1979, the rampant use of the adhesive almost caused quarterback Mark Herrmann to come unglued.

After Herrmann hit tight end and team Most Valuable Player Dave Young over the middle for a short gain, Herrmann went back to the well on the next play. This time, however, when Herrmann tried to pass the ball there was so much stick-um on it that it merely trickled from his right arm, dribbling to the artificial surface at Kinnick Stadium.

Herrmann, not known for his emotional outbursts, grabbed his receiving corps on the sidelines and said, "I want that stuff off your hands by the next time we get the ball." Stuff wasn't exactly the word Herrmann used, however.

Young, Bart Burrell, Raymond Smith and the others knew "Herm" wasn't kidding. So one by one, they got the "gunk" off their hands, and one by one, they went over to show their quarterback they were "gunk free."

Purdue got out of the sticky situation with a 20-14 win, helping Purdue to its top single-season victory total in school history with 10 wins.

"The Voice" and "The Rock"

John DeCamp and Henry Rosenthal were Purdue's answer to the Odd Couple.

DeCamp, known as the "Voice of Purdue," was the Boilermakers' play-by-play man for five decades on WBAA and the Purdue Radio Network. Though he possessed a terrific wit, he was extremely meticulous with his radio preparation and had conservative views that would have made Rush Limbaugh proud.

Rosenthal was a little more flamboyant. A shrewd businessman, he made his lifelong dream of being a broadcaster and owning a radio station a reality. He was the owner of the Lafayette area station WASK that originated its own radio broadcasts of Purdue sports from 1961 to 1982. He flew his own airplane and escorted many Purdue athletics department dignitaries in the 1960s and '70s. He didn't have the voice of DeCamp, but he matched his passion for radio.

Rosenthal, however, had another nickname, "The Rock," that was born years earlier. It was given to him by basketball great Herman Gilliam in the Los Angeles airport when Purdue was on its way to Hawaii for the 1968 Rainbow Classic.

Rosenthal, who was chatting with Gilliam and star guard Billy Keller while awaiting the flight, spotted television star Milton Berle walking through the airport. Never one to be shy, Rosenthal got out his tape recorder, introduced himself to Berle and asked him for an interview to be aired on a later Purdue broadcast.

Once the interview concluded, Rosenthal rejoined Gilliam and Keller. Gilliam, impressed with Rosenthal's ability to get the interview, said, "You are the rock, a regular Rock Hudson."

The nickname stuck.

"The Rock" and "The Voice" were roommates on numerous trips for a number of years. Neither, however, would own up to the origination of the nicknames "Dummy One" and "Dummy Two" that were given to the broadcast duo by members of the Purdue athletics department and basketball travel party over the years.

CHAPTER 5

1980s

Fired Up for IU

Lee Rose was a Southern gentleman with a sharp tongue. Almost like an evangelist in his delivery, he had a way of getting his message across to his team but rarely, if ever, used foul language in front of his squad.

After the Boilermakers disposed of St. John's 87-70 in the second round of the 1980 NCAA Tournament played at Mackey Arena, Rose had a few select words for their next opponent—Big Ten champion Indiana.

"I don't like Indiana, and I don't think you do either," Rose said to his team. "Everyone is going to tell you this week that you don't have a chance against IU. But let me tell you one thing, we are going to beat Indiana and we are going to beat them handily. We've got work to do before that happens, but I know we will get it done."

Rose proved prophetic, as the Boilermakers defeated Bob Knight's Hoosiers 76-69 five days later in Lexington, Kentucky. And the game was not as close as the seven-point score indicated.

Why Lee Left

L ee Rose, who led Purdue to a Big Ten title and a trip to
the NCAA Final Four in two years as head coach of the
Boilermaker basketball team from 1978 to 1980, never was totally
comfortable in West Lafayette.

He came to Purdue from UNC-Charlotte, where he took the
49ers to the Final Four in 1977. He inherited just two starters,
Joe Barry Carroll and Jerry Sichting, from a team that had grossly
underachieved the previous season in Coach Fred Schaus's final
year.

Rose did a remarkable job of building the team around Carroll
and turning the Boilermaker program, which had been a fast-
break team for decades, into a halfcourt, defensive-oriented club.

Rose, who never had been at a school that had a big-time
football program, didn't like sharing the spotlight. And, at the
time, the Boilermakers of the gridiron were enjoying a resurgence
under Coach Jim Young that included three consecutive bowl
appearances from 1978 to 1980. Rose never understood why the
football program had access to some resources that the basketball
program didn't.

Rose also loathed recruiting. And he was struggling with that
part of the job in his short tenure at Purdue. Finishing second
for Chicago prep stars Terry Cummings and Teddy Grubbs and
having to play second fiddle to Indiana's Bob Knight with in-state
players brought that disenchantment to the forefront.

When the 1980 season came to a close, Rose's franchise player
Joe Barry Carroll was graduating, and there was little evidence of
Rose's recruiting success on campus to entice him to stay. George
Steinbrenner, who was involved with the fledgling basketball
program at the University of South Florida in addition to being
principal owner of the New York Yankees, came at Rose with a
$10,000 bonus and the promise of no football with which to
compete.

The offer was too good for Rose to pass up. Some in the
Purdue athletics administration also were weary of Rose's

unhappiness and some were privately glad to see him go, but Rose's departure left many of the Boilermaker faithful wondering what kind of coach would be happy at Purdue.

It didn't take long for an answer, however. Athletics director George King found someone who really wanted the job and who wouldn't use Purdue as a stepping stone to better and more lucrative college basketball jobs. That person was Gene Keady.

Football Junkie

Coach Jim Young was always obsessed with the game of football. He spent countless hours watching game film. Some called him a workaholic who outprepared everybody.

A couple of years after Young had left the Purdue sidelines in 1981, he took the job at West Point as Army's head coach. He asked Boilermaker receiver Bart Burrell to join his coaching staff as receivers coach. Burrell passed on the invitation, but it was during a 1983 visit to West Point when he learned just how fixated Young was on the game.

The New York area had recently been hit by a blizzard. When Burrell arrived, he noticed that the hair above the ankles on Young's legs looked like it had been shaved off. Apparently, the snow was so deep that Young wasn't able to drive to his office and he was forced to battle the frigid temperatures on foot. Instead of putting on boots, he just conquered the drifts in his loafers. There was film to watch and Young wasn't going to let a little snow get in his way. A mild case of frostbite had taken the hair off Young's legs but still hadn't slowed his preparation.

Burrell also recalled that Young's family had yet to relocate and his house was unfurnished. Its contents consisted of a mattress on the floor, a film projector and a sheet on the wall that served as a screen.

"I can just picture him going to the office and every night coming home and watching film," Burrell said.

"He told his wife [Jane] he took the [Arizona assistant coaching position in 1992] because he wouldn't have to work as hard. Still, during the season, he never got home until midnight. He didn't know any other way."

Fred Found Gene

When men's basketball coach Lee Rose left Purdue for the University of South Florida in April of 1980, the Boilermakers began their search for a successor. George King always worked from a short list of candidates that some of his staff kept on hand for him. On the heels of a trip to the Final Four a month earlier, King and Co. contacted some of the top names in college basketball to see if they were interested in the position. Terry Holland of Virginia was one of many hot properties at the time who expressed some interest in the job.

Word in the college basketball community at the time was that the Purdue opportunity was a graveyard job because of the fact that the Boilermakers always would have to play second fiddle to Bob Knight at Indiana.

Fred Schaus, who coached basketball at Purdue before Rose, was a senior administrator on King's staff. He had met Gene Keady at the National Sports Festival in Colorado Springs, Colorado, the year before. He loved the way Keady worked with the kids and kept an eye on him as Keady entered what would be his second and final year at Western Kentucky University.

When the time came to interview Keady, King and Schaus found a coach who wasn't too worried about Knight. In fact, Keady admitted in the interview that he liked the IU coach's philosophy regarding toughness and graduating players. He admired Knight's dogged commitment to winning, as well. He also told the search committee that he would not back down to anyone if he got the job at Purdue.

Keady drove all night to get to the job interview. And despite a phone call to NBC analyst Al McGuire that resulted in McGuire advising Keady not to take the Purdue job, it wasn't long before King and Schaus knew they had the right man for the job.

Joe Barry Gives Roses

J oe Barry Carroll, a 1980 All-America center as a senior at Purdue and No. 1 pick of the Golden State Warriors in the NBA draft, rarely spoke to the press. That left many people with the impression that he was aloof or just didn't care.

"I have nothing to say to the media that is newsworthy," Carroll would say.

Carroll had plenty to say—it just wasn't to the media.

He had a quiet disposition but was blessed with a great sense of humor. His teammates loved him for his wit and the fact that there was a lot more to him than his abilities on the basketball court. He was astute enough to practically negotiate his own deal with Golden State, and since the conclusion of his NBA days, he has made a great living in the financial services business in Atlanta.

It took till the last regular-season game of his playing career for fans to see the emotional side of Carroll. With 40 seconds left and the Boilermakers holding an 18-point lead against defending national champion Michigan State, Carroll went to the bench with a thunderous ovation for the last time after a sterling 26-point, 13-rebound performance. The school's all-time leading rebounder and second all-time scorer had said his goodbye to the Mackey Arena crowd.

But Carroll was far from finished. He ran to the end of the bench where the managers had stored a box of roses. After grabbing the box, he hustled across the court to greet his teary-eyed mother, who was sitting in the pit across the court from the Spartans' bench. In his biggest emotional outburst as a player, Carroll starting waving his arms, imploring the crowd to stand and cheer. The crowd responded with one of the loudest ovations ever heard in Mackey.

Tears flowed freely in the crowd, with coach Lee Rose among

the most noticeably emotional. Rose had received the blessing of Michigan State coach Jud Heathcote before the game to stop the game for the presentation. Heathcote was a willing participant since he had brought Magic Johnson into Jenison Fieldhouse when the Boilermakers were in town for the Big Ten opener earlier that year, briefly interrupting the game.

Carroll's presentation was just the emotional lift the Boilermakers needed as they won five NCAA games en route to a third-place finish in the 1980 Big Dance.

Recruiting Russell

Gene Keady's recruiting ability was tested a few hours after he took the coaching job at Purdue in 1980. Departed coach Lee Rose left the talent cupboard relatively bare when he took off for the University of South Florida. Keady quickly inked Fort Wayne's Greg Eifert and Ricky Hall. He also added Jon Lawson from his former home of Bowling Green, Kentucky. In addition, Joe Gampfer, a seven-foot center from Cincinnati, had committed under Rose's watch and agreed to join Keady.

The big prize, McDonald's All-American Russell Cross from Chicago Manley High School, still was unsigned. Prior to leaving Purdue, Rose got the inside track on Cross's services by inviting him to Purdue's campus to participate as a high school member of the Spartakiade team that toured the Soviet Union in the summer of 1979.

After Rose left Purdue, Keady had some patching up to do. Still, he liked his chances. Cross's high school coach, Willie Little, called Keady at home at midnight the night before Cross was going to make the announcement. Little informed Keady that there was a problem and he needed to see the coach immediately. Keady, not thrilled about his second all-night drive in a period of a couple of days, nearly wrecked his car while driving to Chicago through a rainstorm. Keady and Little met on the south side of

Gene Keady

Chicago, and the new Boilermaker boss learned that Cross might be headed elsewhere.

The story gets a little more bizarre from there.

Later that morning, Keady went to the radio station where Cross was to make his announcement. Cross entered the studio wearing a Purdue cap and T-shirt. Keady presumed all was well until Cross started talking. With the news cameras rolling and the radio airwaves filled, Cross promptly announced he was headed to college at Illinois-Chicago Circle. Coincidentally, Little had just been named assistant coach at Chicago Circle.

Visibly upset, Keady promptly left the press conference and headed back to West Lafayette.

Cross's mother, Annie, was listening to her son's announcement on the radio. She set Cross straight when he got home. Less than 72 hours later, Cross became Purdue's fifth and final recruit.

Prayers Unanswered

Coach Jim Young built the Purdue football program to its highest level in his five-year tenure heading into the 1980 season and the opener against Notre Dame. To show what a big deal the Purdue-Notre Dame matchup was that year, ABC had the game moved up three weeks to September 6 for national television. That kind of switching wasn't done much in those days, and the annual battle between the intrastate rivals was to be the showcase game to kickoff the network television schedule.

Purdue entered the game ranked ninth and the host Fighting Irish ranked 11th. The Boilermakers, who were fresh off their first 10-win season in school annals, had everything on the line. Senior quarterback Mark Herrmann was a leading preseason candidate for the Heisman Trophy, and Purdue was looking to contend for the national title.

But in the days leading up to the game, disaster struck. Herrmann injured the thumb on his right throwing hand on the helmet of an overzealous DSAA (Dummy Scrimmage All-American). That is, a scout team player trying to get the attention of the coaches by making a big play in practice.

There was a great deal of secrecy surrounding whether Herrmann was going to play or not. Herrmann's teammates didn't even know for sure. The medical staff went so far as to numb the thumb of Bob DeMoss, a former great quarterback and quarterbacks coach at Purdue who was a senior athletics department official at the time, to test whether the ball could be thrown without feeling in the thumb.

Herrmann tried to take snaps all the way up to kickoff, but he couldn't go. On the way to the locker room, the deflated Purdue squad prepared for Young's speech.

In the land of Rockne, the Boilermaker coach found it necessary to pull out all the stops to assure his team that things were going to be all right without its star quarterback. What the Boilermakers received from their coach was as close to fire and brimstone as they ever heard from him.

"We aren't going to do anything different," said Young, who started true freshman Scott Campbell in Herrmann's place. "We're going to win this game on the road to the national championship."

Young was trying to get the players to believe in themselves as he turned up the volume on his pregame speech. As Young concluded his talk, he asked his players to take a knee and pray.

In retrospect, that is when the Boilermakers knew they were in trouble. Young had *never* asked them to take a knee in his previous 35 games as head coach.

Young and the Boilermakers found Notre Dame Stadium a tough place to ask for divine intervention for the first time. The Irish won going away, 31-10.

Let Him Play

D r. Loyal "Bill" Combs was an institution in Purdue sports medicine. He also was quite a character. A former standout Purdue football player, Combs's bedside manner often included a dash of toughness with a heaping dose of humor.

In 1981, as the Purdue baseball team was preparing for its first appearance in the Big Ten Tournament, Boilermaker first baseman Greg Beno, a walk-on from Munster, Indiana, went to see Combs with head coach David Alexander about an injured finger.

Combs examined Beno and wasn't too optimistic about Beno's chances to play. He thought that Beno might be risking future use of the finger if he hurt it again.

"Is this kid a pro prospect?" Combs whispered to Alexander off to the side of the examining table out of the earshot of Beno.

"No," Alexander said. "He is a great kid, but his playing days are over after he is done here."

"Oh, what the hell then," the gruff Combs said. "Let him play."

A Surprise Departure

A fter resurrecting the Boilermaker football program from 1977 to 1981, compiling a 38-19-1 record (26-14-1 in the Big Ten), Coach Jim Young surprisingly resigned following the 1981 season for family reasons. It was a decision he told athletics director George King about before the 1981 season began.

Contrary to what some may believe, Young said he was always happy with his situation in West Lafayette and left coaching to gain athletics administration experience.

"I've always done what I felt was right at the particular time," Young said. "I enjoyed coaching at Purdue very much. At the time I got out I had spent a lot of time on the program and put a lot into it. I thought I should explore other possibilities, perhaps going the athletics director route. I certainly wasn't unhappy at Purdue."

When Fred Schaus left for West Virginia, the opportunity came along for Young to be named an associate athletics director at Purdue.

"Pursuing an athletics directorship didn't excite me as much as I thought it might," Young said. "I never assumed I would be the athletics director at Purdue. I assumed I would get a couple of years' experience there as associate AD and move on.

"When the West Point job opened it appealed to me. When I told my wife she said, 'You're crazy. Why aren't you still at Purdue?'"

Young liked the idea of working with outstanding young cadets. In addition, he had been a military buff all of his life. Young also said his decision to leave the Boilermaker program wasn't based on speculation that the program was on the decline.

"I don't think it was headed down when you had two pro quarterbacks as a freshman and sophomore at that particular time [Scott Campbell and Jim Everett]," he said. "If anything I felt the program was in pretty good shape."

Everett Almost Ended Up at Tight End

Quarterback Jim Everett, who finished sixth in the Heisman Trophy voting following his senior season at Purdue in 1985, almost was a tight end.

Lightly recruited out of Albuquerque, New Mexico, he eventually picked Purdue over Stanford, but was almost never given a chance to prove his worth under center. After the coach who recruited him, Jim Young, quit at Purdue in 1981, Everett worried about who would guide the team. It bothered him to the point that he considered transferring, but assistant coach Bob Spoo talked him out of it. When assistant Leon Burtnett, the defensive coordinator, was promoted to the head coaching position, Everett's fears subsided somewhat. That is, until it was mentioned that he might become a tight end.

"Coach Spoo and I had a lot of long talks about what my future would hold," Everett said. "There was one point when he and Coach Burtnett thought it might be better for me to become a tight end. I wasn't very happy about it and wanted them to give me another chance to show what I could do on the field. Thankfully, they did."

Fat and Slow Is No Way to Go Through Life

The Boilermakers and second-year coach Gene Keady were getting pounded by Bob Knight's Hoosiers in Bloomington in 1982. The game was nearing the end, and the Hoosiers, who were leading by 20 points, found themselves going through the motions.

Purdue sophomore center Joe Gampfer, who was on the long road back from a crippling knee injury, was inserted into the game in the closing minutes. Gampfer, one of the most likeable guys on the team, was battling the beltline and was at least 50 pounds overweight. The seven-footer from Cincinnati had soft hands and an excellent shooting touch, and on the next to the last possession of the game, he got the ball in the post and went right around IU center Uwe Blab for an easy lay-in and was fouled.

Knight, like Keady, never was one to stop coaching no matter what the score. The fact that the game no longer was in doubt didn't matter to either coach. The Assembly Hall partisan crowd had gone quiet with the battle long since won, so Knight took this opportunity to make a point to Blab as he ran down the court.

"How could you let that fat [pause], slow [pause], son of a b—— [pause] score on you like that?" bellowed Knight across the court.

Knight's speech was so deliberate and pronounced that everyone within several feet of the IU bench could hear him. When Knight sat down on the bench, murmurs of laughter could be heard behind both team benches.

Had Gampfer heard Knight say it, he would have laughed, too, as he possessed one of the best senses of humor on the team.

1,000 x 2

The women's basketball program had 18 players score 1,000 career points through the 2002-03 season. Ironically, the first two to reach the coveted plateau did so in the same game.

It was February 27, 1982, and the Boilermakers were playing host to Central Michigan. Women's basketball was in just its seventh season as a varsity sport at Purdue. Junior Carol Emanuel became the first player to score 1,000 points and soon was followed by senior Sue Bartz.

Nancy Cross, then an assistant coach under Ruth Jones, recalled years later the accomplishment(s) being a big deal.

"I remember that they stopped the game and presented Carol with a ball, and a few minutes later they stopped it again for Sue," Cross said. "There were maybe 300 people in the stands, and they were mostly people who were pretty close to the players, so it meant something. People talked about what an impressive accomplishment it was for two players to score 1,000 points for a program that was relatively new."

Emanuel later became the first women's basketball player to be inducted into the Purdue Intercollegiate Athletics Hall of Fame.

"The neatest thing about Carol is if you had asked her, she would not have had any idea how many points she had, nor would she have cared," Cross said. "In fact, when they stopped the game to make the announcement about her 1,000th point, I remember Carol saying to Ruth, 'Why are we stopping the game? Let's just keep playing.'"

Class Act

E ven in defeat, men's basketball coach Gene Keady almost always has acted with class. And the same can be said about the legendary Boilermaker boss even when he was on the short end of recruiting battles.

Following the 1981-82 season, Keady invited Steve Alford, who at the time was a junior-to-be at New Castle High School, and his father, Sam, the head coach at New Castle, to speak at one of his summer basketball camps. Why was this out of the ordinary? Because Alford had already verbally committed to Bob Knight's Indiana Hoosiers.

It was a move that Alford, who became an All-American, national champion and Olympic gold medalist, as well as a successful college head coach, remembers to this day.

"I remember going up there my junior year to speak at a clinic," recalled Alford, who was named Indiana's Mr. Basketball following the 1982-83 season. "My dad spoke and I did an individual workout. I had already committed to Indiana and obviously everybody knows the rivalry between Indiana and Purdue. So here was somebody that had already committed to the opposite end of the rival, yet Coach Keady had Dad and me in to speak at a summer camp. He spent time with us in his office, and I'll never forget that because I just thought that was a very classy gesture on his part.

"He's somebody that I've continued to watch and follow just because his teams play so hard, have a great work ethic they have and great attitude towards the game. The passion that they have to play the game has always been something that I think all young coaches try to emulate."

One That Got Away

F ormer Boilermaker All-Big Ten linebacker and current defensive coordinator Brock Spack will never forget

Purdue's 35-31 loss to Wisconsin on October 2, 1982, in Ross-Ade Stadium.

With the Badgers out of timeouts, quarterback Scott Campbell inexplicably ran out of bounds to stop the clock with under a minute left. Campbell tried to spend time stalling out the clock, but got too close to the sidelines and was pushed to the boundary by Badger defenders.

Facing a fourth-down situation, Purdue elected to punt. Wisconsin's Dave Mielke blocked Matt Kinzer's punt and returned it 34 yards for a touchdown with just 30 seconds left for the game-winning score, which stunned the sellout crowd of 69,132.

"That was the most unbelievable loss I've ever been associated with," Spack said. "I still can't believe it. That left a big scar.

"We had a two-touchdown lead [24-10 with 9:39 left in the third quarter] and gave up a score late in the fourth quarter [that trimmed Purdue's lead to 31-29 with 1:29 to play]. All we had to do is run the clock.

"I've talked to some guys who are acquaintances of mine who were on the field for the Badgers about that game. [Badger starting quarterback] Randy Wright still says that is the most incredible win he's ever been associated with."

Head Coach Leon Burtnett was as disappointed as anybody as the loss dropped his team to 0-4 on the season.

"It wouldn't have been so bad, but we had called timeout right before that and had talked about that [not running out of bounds]," Burtnett said. "I told him [Campbell] to make sure not to cross the hash mark and when he did we could see that there could be a potential problem."

Even the mistake by long snapper Pat Snyder was very much out of the ordinary.

"Pat never had another bad snap in his whole career," Burtnett recalled. "When I was with the Indianapolis Colts and we had replacement players [in the mid-1980s], Pat came in and snapped the ball for us, and he snapped during two regular-season games [following the strike]. He still snaps the ball every year for the punters [at the NFL Combine in Indianapolis], so to this day he's still snapping the ball."

Nearly Perfect

The 1982 volleyball team won its first 33 matches, capturing the third of its four Big Ten championships along the way. The Boilermakers were pushed to five games only twice during the regular season, October 2 at Minnesota and October 20 at Illinois State.

After winning their first-round match in the NCAA Tournament in four games over Rutgers, the Boilermakers played host to Nebraska in the Mideast Regional semifinals on December 11. It proved to be one of the greatest matches in school history.

The Cornhuskers opened a 2-0 lead, winning by identical 15-12 scores, before Purdue stormed back with 15-4, 15-12 and 15-5 decisions to keep its perfect record in tact. Junior Joan King erupted for 30 kills on a .464 hitting percentage, while senior Jane Neff had 19 kills and sophomore Kate Crandell tallied 16 kills, 11 blocks and four service aces.

Next up was a date with defending national champion USC in the regional finals the following day, and the Trojans proved to be too much, sweeping the Boilermakers 15-13, 15-3, 15-8 to end their dream season at 33-1. USC went on to lose to Hawaii in the NCAA title match in five games.

An Unlikely Hero

Boilermaker center Jim Rowinski capped the greatest comeback in Purdue basketball history.

The six-foot-eight New York native banked in a top-of-the-key jumper with one second left, giving Purdue a 56-54 win on February 23, 1983, at Illinois.

"It was not the play that was designed," admitted Steve Reid, a sophomore guard on the team. "Row improvised a little bit. He always thought of himself as a guard anyway. I think that was the longest shot he attempted in his career."

Not to anyone's surprise, Rowinski didn't call, "Bank."

As a matter of fact, at the next day's practice his teammates made him try to bank some free throws and they weren't close.

The Boilermakers weren't close midway through the second half in Champaign. They trailed 49-29 and tallied the game's final 18 points in the last 9:38 to pull out the unforgettable win.

Coach Gene Keady was so fed up with the way his team was playing that he benched some of his key players (Curt Clawson, Reid, Greg Eifert and Dan Palombizio). He replaced them with four players who had played a combined 122 minutes in 12 Big Ten games. All-everything center Russell Cross remained on the floor and was joined by Mack Gadis, Herb Robinson, Rowinski and Ted Benson.

Point guard Ricky Hall replaced Benson at the eight-minute mark, but Purdue still trailed 54-41. With just under five minutes to go, Robinson's three-pointer from the left wing knotted the score at 54. Keady thought about putting all of his starters back in, but opted not to.

"I was the biggest cheerleader there was in Assembly Hall," Reid recalled. "Coming back from 20 doesn't sound like a lot, but there was no shot clock in those days.

"Ricky Hall and Russell Cross played. Don't let anybody tell you otherwise. Coach knew, 'I can go so far, but I've got to have those two on the floor.'"

Illinois held the ball and was trying to get the last shot, but Hall stripped Illini guard Derek Harper with three ticks left and called timeout, which set up Rowinski's heroics.

The Long Road for "Row"

Jim Rowinski came to Purdue from Syosset, New York, as a six-foot-four, 190-pound walk-on in the fall of 1979. He graduated as a 6'8", 255-pound center who led Purdue to a share of the Big Ten men's basketball title in 1984.

The road was far from easy for Rowinski. As a true freshman, he served as a member of Coach Lee Rose's "Renegade" or demonstration squad. After Rose departed following that season, the Long Island native grew four inches and began to bulk up a little. In Coach Gene Keady's first year, Rowinski made the traveling squad as an end-of-the-bench walk-on.

Rowinski took a lot of abuse from some players on Keady's first team. Having grown three inches since coming to Purdue, he didn't have many clothes that fit. The shy but likeable Rowinski took the ribbing in stride and just kept plugging.

The following season, Rowinski had bulked up to 235 pounds. His progress as a player continued as he won the starting job at center for the Sugar Bowl Tournament in December of 1981 in New Orleans against Houston. The Cougars, who would make it to the Final Four that year, had an extremely raw player at center, too, by the name of Hakeem Olajuwon.

Unfortunately, Rowinski suffered a stress fracture in his foot in New Orleans and missed the rest of the season. But the distance he had come just to get to start against Olajuwon was remarkable.

Two years later, in his only season as a full-time starter, Rowinski was named the Big Ten Most Valuable Player in one of the most astonishing rags-to-riches stories in conference history.

Proximity Pays Dividends

Of all of Coach Gene Keady's recruiting classes, the 1983-84 class is arguably the best.

Landing the three marquee players in the class—Troy Lewis, Todd Mitchell and Everette Stephens—proved to be a major coup for Keady and his coaching staff.

Had it not been for Purdue's close proximity to his hometown of Anderson, Indiana, Lewis would have ended up at Kansas. In addition to Purdue, he visited UCLA, Illinois, Duke and Kansas.

Lewis, Indiana's 1984 co-Mr. Basketball, often talks about how impressed he was with Jayhawk coach Larry Brown's recruiting pitch, saying he might have inked with Kansas at a

Lawrence ice cream parlor had Brown pulled out the national letter of intent on the spot.

Mitchell, a Toledo, Ohio, native, took trips to Purdue, UCLA, Minnesota and Pittsburgh. He liked UCLA, but didn't hit it off with some of the Panther players and thought Minneapolis was too cold. In the end, he decided Purdue was the place for him since it was not an unreasonable drive for his parents. He had also developed a friendship with Lewis on a recruiting trip to UCLA that gave him extra incentive to go to school where his newfound buddy was headed.

Purdue, in particular assistant coach Bruce Weber, got in on Stephens early. The native of Evanston, Illinois, visited Purdue, Iowa, Kentucky and Evansville. However, he wasn't the top guard on Iowa or Kentucky's lists, and Evansville was a mid-major that didn't interest him too much.

After Weber saw Stephens's high school practice, he told Keady to drive up and see him the next day. Keady did and reportedly locked Stephens in his car until Stephens said yes. Two days later, Stephens committed to Purdue.

"Pac-Mac" Opens Doors

On October 29, 1985, Purdue promotions director Nancy Cross sweat blood trying to bring all the pieces together to break an NCAA attendance record for women's volleyball. Through an incredible effort by many, it came to fruition as 10,645 fans packed Mackey Arena to see Carol Dewey's nationally prominent volleyball team defeat Western Michigan.

In many ways, the event paved the way for the support in terms of increased attendance that women's basketball would begin to enjoy under Coach Lin Dunn a few years later. It proved to all that there was support for women's sports at Purdue and that in the right situation fans would come in droves to see the product. In the years since Pac-Mac, it has been proven over and over again.

Troy Makes His, Todd Doesn't

The life lessons of playing basketball for Coach Gene Keady endure. Keady has preached throughout his tenure that having the discipline to do the little things like making one's bed leads to success.

Troy Lewis willingly followed Keady's instructions (sometimes due to a pinch of fear) pretty much to the letter.

Todd Mitchell, Lewis's classmate on Big Ten championship teams in 1987 and 1988, always wrestled to some extent with Keady and his disciplinary teachings. Keady reminded Mitchell of his demanding father, and that was good in some ways and not in others.

Fifteen years removed from his playing days, Lewis admits he makes his bed every day. Mitchell, still with a trace of defiance, doesn't.

A Dedication to Remember

The September 8, 1984, football game between Purdue and Notre Dame served as the dedication game for Indianapolis's Hoosier Dome. As far as Boilermaker fans were concerned, they couldn't have written a better script to initiate the new indoor football facility.

The contest was originally scheduled to be a home game for Notre Dame, but the Fighting Irish brass elected to move the contest from Notre Dame Stadium to the capital city. They're still regretting that decision today.

On paper, the game, which was played in front of a sellout crowd of 60,672 that was deafening at times, was supposed to be nothing more than a tune-up for the eighth-ranked Irish. Purdue was an 18-point underdog.

However, the prognosticators forgot to tell the Boilermakers, as they stunned the partisan Notre Dame crowd with a 23-21 victory.

"That game was great," Purdue head coach Leon Burtnett recalled. "Everything was set for them. When we went down there to work out, they didn't turn on the lights for us. Notre Dame came in right after us and they turned on the lights for them.

"That was their home game and supposed to be their big victory. We played extremely well."

"I would be less than honest if I said I liked our chances going into the game," admitted Joe Tiller, who was Purdue's assistant head coach, defensive coordinator and defensive line coach at the time. "They had a very, very talented football team, many of whom went on to the NFL. Our best players were young, like sophomore Rod Woodson.

"What I also remember about the game besides the fact that we won was standing in the tunnel next to Fred Strickland, who was a true freshman. I recruited Fred the year before out of New Jersey. I looked up at Fred and said, 'Fred, a year ago did you think you would be standing here getting ready to play your first college football game against Notre Dame, and you're going to play in it?' He couldn't talk [he was so excited]. He just shook his head."

Purdue trailed 14-3 after the first quarter, but trimmed the deficit to 14-13 by halftime. The Boilermakers took the lead for good on a 20-yard field goal by Mike Rendina with 3:47 left in the third quarter. Purdue increased its lead to 23-14 with just under 14 minutes remaining in the game when quarterback Jim Everett hooked up with flanker Jeff Price for a 14-yard scoring strike. Irish tailback Allen Pinkett scored on a six-yard run with 4:21 to go to draw the Blue and Gold to within two, but the Boilermakers' Don Baldwin intercepted an ill-advised screen pass by Irish quarterback Steve Buerlein late in the game to pull off the upset.

The victory secured the starting job for Everett. It was a game-time decision to give the nod to Everett over redshirt freshman quarterback Doug Downing. Everett, however, never looked back, leading Purdue to the Peach Bowl and becoming one of the most prolific passers in Big Ten history.

Hat Trick

Indeed 1984 was a football season to remember for the Purdue faithful. That was the year the Boilermakers defeated Notre Dame, Ohio State and Michigan in the same season, which put the Old Gold and Black in elite company. Michigan State, in 1951 and 1965, was the only other school in the nation to have defeated the Fighting Irish, Buckeyes and Wolverines in the same season.

Both the Irish and Buckeyes were ranked when Purdue faced them. Michigan was unranked but was under the direction of legendary coach Bo Schembechler. Purdue led Michigan, which went on to lose to BYU in the Holiday Bowl giving the Cougars a national championship, 24-0 at halftime and held on for a 31-29 victory.

Boilermaker coach Leon Burtnett called that first half against Michigan "the greatest half of football we ever played."

A Difference of Opinion

Purdue was 4-0 in bowl games entering the Peach Bowl on December 31, 1984, but that undefeated mark was ruined thanks to quarterback Don "Magic Man" Majkowski and his Virginia Cavaliers, who mounted a second-half comeback.

The Boilermakers looked to be in complete control of the game as they scored two touchdowns in a span of just 81 seconds late in the second quarter to lead 24-14.

Coach Leon Burtnett and offensive coordinator Jim Colletto, however, butted heads just prior to halftime on the Boilermakers' strategy.

"Jim had a tendency to forget who the head coach was at times," Burtnett admitted. "I wanted to call timeout and try to score [again in the final minute of the half]. When you've got Jim Everett and that group, you're expected to score points."

Joe Tiller, who was the Boilermakers' assistant head coach

and defensive coordinator at the time, said Burtnett and Colletto definitely weren't on the same page.

"They had a disagreement," Tiller said. "I didn't get involved in it. We had our hands full defensively.

"I wasn't happy with the offense because I thought we were doing everything we could do defensively to contain a very talented Virginia team, and we were on the field too much. We were beginning to wear down. I knew if we didn't get some help by controlling the ball and doing some things offensively ... I was just hoping our offense would do a better job because the strength of our team at that time was the offense with Everett and those guys. I thought, 'If these guys perform at the same level that we performed at during the season, we can win this thing,' but they were underperforming at the time. I thought, 'If we continue to underperform, we're not going to win.'"

Virginia scored 13 unanswered points in the second half to win the game.

"We just blew the second half," Burtnett said. "Offensively, we just stunk up the second half. We did not play well at all."

Purdue finished with 328 yards, including 75 yards rushing on 21 carries. Virginia had 392 yards, including 274 yards rushing on 64 carries. Everett completed 22 of 42 passes for 253 yards with three touchdowns and three interceptions, while Majkowski was eight of 17 for 118 yards passing with one touchdown and two interceptions.

Due in part to his fallout with Burtnett, Colletto left the Purdue staff to become Arizona State's offensive coordinator. Burtnett promoted Bob Spoo to be the Boilermakers' offensive coordinator.

Watch Out for That Chair

Indiana coach Bob Knight had had it with some of the calls made by the officiating crew in the Purdue-IU game February 23, 1985, in Assembly Hall and showed his disgust in the opening minutes of the contest by throwing a red chair from the Hoosier bench across the floor.

Guard Steve Reid was preparing to shoot free throws as a result of Knight's first technical, but before he shot the ball, the chair came flying by him.

"The ref gave me the ball and I started to go through my free throw routine. I was getting ready to dribble and it came flying across," Reid said. "The first thing that crossed my mind was, 'That has to be another technical.'"

The infamous chair toss did lead to another technical foul assessed to Knight—and his ejection.

"The thing I recall, and Coach [Gene] Keady doesn't remember this but I do because it has permanently scarred me, is that I made three out of the six free throws [two for each technical and two for a personal foul that was called] and then we had a timeout," Reid said. "Coach used the whole timeout to pretty much question my leadership ability as a senior and told me that making three out of six is ridiculous. As we ended our huddle he said, 'If we lose this game, Reid, it's your fault.'

"Had we lost, I would've had to move to Alaska or Siberia."

Purdue won the game 72-63.

Following the Boilermaker win, Keady, who respected Knight's coaching success but didn't care for his temper tantrums or antics, emphatically reminded the media that the Purdue victory was the story.

Knight had berated the Boilermaker program in Keady's first season, complaining of the "Purdue mentality," but after the chair-throwing incident, the media gave the Boilermakers credit for running a program that was conducted with class regardless of the outcome of games.

No Food for You

During his tenure as Purdue's basketball coach, Gene Keady has made it a tradition to stop at the Beef House in Covington, Indiana (just four miles from the Indiana-Illinois state line), on the way to and or from games at the University of Illinois.

The players look forward to the event because it is a guaranteed sensational meal. One trip to the Beef House, however, would like to be forgotten by the 1984-85 Boilermakers, but never will be.

Purdue headed to 18th-ranked Illinois after beating Indiana the game before, in the famous Bob Knight chair-throwing game at Assembly Hall. The Boilermakers had easily handled the fifth-ranked Fighting Illini a month earlier 54-34 in Mackey Arena.

However, Coach Lou Henson's Illini were ready to ambush the Boilermakers, sensing Purdue might have a letdown after the emotional win over Indiana. Illinois's intuition was correct, as it administered one of the worst beatings in the Keady era, doubling Purdue 86-43.

Even after the drubbing, the team was looking to ease its sorrows with some fine red meat midway through its two-hour bus ride back to West Lafayette.

Legend had it that Keady stopped at the popular restaurant, picked up his team's order and sat with it up front on the bus. After a few miles, he threw it out the window.

But that's not really what happened.

Starting guard Steve Reid remembers the incident vividly.

"One of the things you always looked forward to going to Illinois for was stopping at the Beef House and having a nice steak," Reid said. "After we got beat by 43 points, we pulled into the Beef House and we kind of stand up to get off the bus. Coach, in his normal voice, said, 'Sit down. You're not getting steak,' using a couple of other words. So we sat down and they started bringing boxes in.

"We got hamburgers with no cheese or condiments, potato chips and warm Pepsi that didn't have any ice. Somebody had the nerve, I don't know if it was a freshman or not, but he stood up and asked one of the managers, 'Do we have any ketchup?' Coach stood up and said, 'None of you need ketchup or deserve ketchup. Now sit your a—es down.'

"If you suffer the second-worst loss in school history, you

don't need ketchup on your food."

The team arrived back at Mackey Arena at 2:30 a.m., and it was off to bed, right? Wrong. Keady told the Boilermakers to get taped and be on the floor in 20 minutes. They practiced until 4 a.m.

Good as Gold

The Boilermakers shocked the Ross-Ade Stadium sellout crowd of 69,748 on November 22, 1986, when they came out for the Old Oaken Bucket game wearing old gold jerseys.

According to Coach Leon Burtnett, the team was not aware that it would wear the jerseys almost until kickoff.

"They didn't know about it until they came back in from warmups," Burtnett said. "About 20 minutes before the game was the first time they ever saw them."

Burtnett said he asked the players for money about three weeks prior to the Indiana game for something special. Each of the players donated $12 so that everyone on the team could keep his jersey after the game.

"When they brought in the gold jerseys, everybody got excited," All-America defensive back Rod Woodson said.

"I hadn't seen our team show that type of emotion and excitement during the entire season. I knew we were going to win."

Wearing the jerseys gave the players an extra psychological boost as Purdue upset Indiana 17-15.

Burtnett, who had resigned a few weeks earlier, was carried off the field on his players' shoulders as he pumped his fist in the air.

Wow Woodson

Before he became a perennial NFL All-Pro performer, Rod Woodson was anchoring the defensive secondary at Purdue from 1983 to 1986. He shared the school career interceptions record for many years until Stuart Schweigert broke it during the 2002 season.

Woodson capped his career in grandiose style against Indiana on November 22, 1986. With the Boilermakers sporting gold uniforms for the first time since the late 1940s, Woodson played both ways in a 17-15 Old Oaken Bucket victory at Ross-Ade Stadium.

Actually, he played all ways. Offensively, Woodson started at tailback for the first time since high school and rushed for a team season-high 93 yards on 15 carries while catching three passes for 67 yards. At his usual cornerback position, he recorded 10 tackles, one pass breakup and one forced fumble. He also returned three punts for 30 yards and two kickoffs for 46 yards. In all, Woodson appeared in an astounding 137 total plays, approximately 90 percent of the game.

"I have never seen a young man play a game like that before," Purdue head coach Leon Burtnett said afterward. "He is unquestionably the best player in the conference. I wouldn't trade anyone in the country for him. I know [Miami quarterback Vinny] Testeverde is a great player, but Rod has done so many good things for us. He's got to be one of the best in the country."

Said Woodson: "I was very tired. It was a long day out there. I don't think I could do this many more times. It wasn't just me out there; it was a definite team game. This game was for Coach Burtnett [who had been forced to resign two weeks prior], and we just wanted to win it for him."

Woodson went on to be named Purdue's Most Valuable Player and a consensus All-American. He was selected by the Pittsburgh Steelers in the first round of the 1987 NFL draft (10th pick overall).

Rod Woodson

Promises Not Kept

Two years after Coach Leon Burtnett led the Boilermakers to the 1984 Peach Bowl and was named Big Ten Coach of the Year, he was forced to resign.

Burtnett, who had a 21-34-1 record in five seasons at Purdue, entered the 1986 season after a disappointing 5-6 1985 campaign, quarterback Jim Everett's senior season. The Boilermakers went 3-8, and Burtnett was done.

He wished his departure from Purdue could have been

different. Burtnett said he didn't feel like he was on the hot seat entering the 1986 campaign.

"Needless to say there were some promises made [to me] that were not kept," Burtnett said. "I was promised that [having to win in 1986] was not the case. The president [Steven Beering] understood that we were going in with a freshman quarterback ... but that's part of coaching.

"We had the best quarterback in the nation [freshman Jeff George]. I know he has taken a lot of heat [over the years], but Jeff was made some promises by the people in the [Purdue] hierarchy when he came to Purdue that things were going to remain stable. When they didn't [remain that way], that's why he pulled out.

"They had never recruited the No. 1 [high school football] player [in the nation according to *USA Today*] in the history of that school, and they might not ever recruit another one."

Kidnapping the Coach

After Leon Burtnett was let go following the 1986 season, Purdue officials began an extensive search for a new football coach. They thought they had found one in Ron Meyer, who spent nearly a decade at Purdue as a player and an assistant coach.

Meyer, who had coached and recruited Southern Methodist University's "Pony Express" of Eric Dickerson and Craig James before coaching the NFL's New England Patriots, had agreed to become the Boilermakers' coach. He was due in West Lafayette from Dallas on a Monday morning flight to sign the papers and have a press conference that afternoon.

Coincidentally, the Indianapolis Colts also were in search of a head coach after Rod Dowhower was canned. General manager Jim Irsay, who played for Meyer at Southern Methodist, was interested in Meyer's services.

Irsay reportedly caught wind that Purdue was about to hire Meyer from a speech to Purdue alumni in Florida that President

Steven Beering had delivered the Friday before. Irsay figured out Meyer's itinerary, jumped on a plane, and intercepted Meyer in Kansas City.

When the plane got to Indianapolis, Meyer had changed his mind. He let Purdue officials know Monday morning. A few days later, Purdue hired Fred Akers.

Running Rod

In addition to his football exploits, Rod Woodson was a track standout. An Olympic-caliber hurdler, he became the first Big Ten athlete to win four conference 55-meter hurdle championships, and he placed second in the NCAA in that event in 1984.

Woodson, who often sported bruised shins due to sometimes running through (rather than over) hurdles, was at his track best during the 1987 Big Ten indoor championships. He was voted Athlete of the Meet for winning his fourth hurdles title as well as the 55-meter dash and placing third in the 300-meter run.

Woodson still holds both Purdue and Lambert Fieldhouse records in the 55-meter hurdles at 7.11 and 7.14 seconds.

Three Coaches,
Three Years: Part I

Purdue went through three women's basketball coaches in three years from 1996 to 1999. That's when Lin Dunn was replaced by Nell Fortner, who yielded a year later to Carolyn Peck. Amazingly, it marked the second time for such a trilogy.

The Boilermakers faced a similar situation in the mid-1980s. First, Dr. Ruth Jones, coach from 1977 to 1986, succumbed to cancer on July 5, 1986. Marsha Reall replaced her 10 days later, but lasted just one season before resigning. Finally, Lin Dunn was hired on July 18, 1987. Dunn coached at Purdue for nine seasons before not having her contract renewed following the 1995-96 campaign and starting the second "three-in-three" circuit.

Trouble on the Line

As a high school senior in 1986-87, women's basketball player Jane Calhoun narrowed her college choices to Rutgers and Purdue. She liked the Atlantic-10 school because it was a top 10 team whose coach, Theresa Grentz, had been an All-America post player and convinced Calhoun she could make her one, too. Purdue was appealing because it was an up-and-coming program and was located just over an hour's drive from her Tipton, Indiana, home.

Calhoun finally settled on Rutgers, but when she went to call Grentz to give her the news, the Calhoun phone line was dead because of a severe thunderstorm that had hit central Indiana. The phone remained out of service for another day, and during that time Calhoun changed her mind in favor of the Boilermakers. Before attempting to call Grentz, Calhoun did get through to coaches at Iowa State and Northwestern—two other schools that were interested in her—and told them she had settled on Rutgers.

Calhoun initially was recruited by Dr. Ruth Jones, who passed away during the summer between Calhoun's junior and senior years of high school. She signed with Marsha Reall but never played for her after Reall resigned in July of 1987. So when Calhoun arrived on the West Lafayette campus later that summer, essentially her third different Purdue coach, Lin Dunn, greeted her.

Thou Shall Not Break Team Rules

O ne of the more humorous tales regarding Boilermaker basketball roommates centers around Stephen Scheffler and John Brugos.

The two were about as opposite as any two of Coach Gene Keady's players have ever been, and they roomed together during their freshman year in 1986-87.

Scheffler was a stickler for team rules imposed by Keady while Brugos was not, and that's putting it nicely.

The two players butted heads over one of those rules. Like many college students, Brugos liked to indulge in an occasional malt beverage or two. Scheffler, on the other hand, was the son of a minister and didn't believe in partaking in adult beverages.

Word has it that on one occasion Brugos had filled the dormitory refrigerator with beer. When Scheffler discovered the beer in their room, which was obviously a violation of team rules as well as a violation of residence hall rules, he threatened Brugos, saying he would inform the coaching staff if the beer wasn't disposed of (immediately).

Not surprisingly, Brugos didn't take Scheffler's threat seriously. One can draw the conclusion that the burly Scheffler told Keady or someone on his staff about the violation since Brugos was seen running the Mackey Arena stairs the following day.

To this day, Scheffler denies he told on his roommate, but he laughs when asked about the tale.

"We were opposites, but we learned to get along quite well," Scheffler said. "It was better when we weren't roommates because I would continually say to myself, 'I'm not getting busted for this, plus this is wrong.' I never tattled on him, but I said, 'John, if push comes to shove, I will push so you better not do this.'"

Dunn Deal

L in Dunn boldly predicted a Big Ten championship in women's basketball in four years when she assumed the Purdue reins on July 18, 1987. Strong words considering the program had finished no better than fifth in the preceding five years of conference double round-robin play.

After three consecutive third-place showings, Dunn proved to be a prophet. The 1990-91 Boilermakers steamrolled through the Big Ten with a record of 17-1 and an average victory margin of 24.4 points. Their lone loss was a 56-53 setback to Iowa on February 8.

The Boilermakers had their first chance to clinch the title on March 1 when Illinois came to Mackey Arena. They made easy work of the Fighting Illini, winning 112-49. The 63-point margin of victory currently ranks as the second largest in school history. Eleven players scored for Purdue, led by senior center Rhonda Mateen with a career-high 28 points. Mateen put an exclamation point on the victory and the championship with a three-pointer (the only attempt of her career) in the game's closing moments.

Prior to Dunn's arrival, Purdue had gone 47-99 against Big Ten teams, a .322 winning percentage. In Dunn's nine seasons, the Boilermakers went 120-38, a .759 winning percentage, including 18-0 against Indiana and 16-0 against Michigan.

Pick Him, Pick Her

W hen Lin Dunn was hired as the women's basketball coach in July of 1987, she inherited two assistants, Tom Collen and Gail Goestenkors. Desiring to keep some continuity on the staff but also wanting to make her own hire, Dunn thought she would keep either Collen or Goestenkors and let the other one go.

Dunn asked both of them who they would keep, and when each said the other, she thought that was endorsement enough

Lin Dunn

to keep both. Together, the three helped put Purdue women's basketball on the map over the next five years.

Goestenkors left the Boilermakers after the 1991-92 season to become head coach at Duke, where she has built the Blue Devils into a national power. Collen left a year later to become an assistant at Arkansas, and later he was hired as head coach at Colorado State. He built the Rams into an NCAA contender and is now head coach at Louisville.

A Spirit Chain
Like no Other

It has been common for Purdue men's basketball tickets to be a hot commodity through the years, but the demand for student season tickets entering the 1987-88 season was unlike any since the days of Rick Mount 20 years earlier.

The Purdue athletic ticket office was caught a little off guard on October 19, 1987, the first day student season tickets went on sale. Thousands of Boilermaker students lined up outside the ticket office. The line was hundreds of yards long and wrapped around half of Mackey Arena by 8 a.m. when the tickets went on sale. At 3 p.m., it was still as long. Students waited an average of four and a half hours in lines of approximately 2,000 people long to get a chance to buy tickets, which were priced at $32 for the season package.

The demand for tickets was so high that an actual lottery had to be held to figure out just who would receive the coveted tickets.

Coach Gene Keady said he didn't even think about what kind of response there would be until he saw the lengthy lines.

"It's a very self-satisfying feeling," Keady said. "We want the students to understand they're our top priority. We really appreciate their loyalty."

Living Up to the Hype

When Coach Gene Keady signed Troy Lewis, Todd Mitchell and Everette Stephens in 1983-84, he had landed one of the top three recruiting classes in the nation.

The trio, which was nicknamed the "Three Amigos"

during their senior season at Purdue by CBS broadcaster Verne Lundquist, didn't disappoint.

During their illustrious collegiate careers, they helped the Boilermakers go 96-28 overall and 53-19 in the Big Ten and capture back-to-back league championships in 1987 and 1988. The goal the trio set for themselves that they failed to achieve was a trip to the Final Four.

Still, the three catapulted Purdue basketball into the national spotlight for two memorable seasons.

The Boilermakers entered the 1986-87 season with a No. 4 ranking in the polls. When they started the season 7-0, *The Sporting News* had them No. 1, while the wire services picked Purdue second.

The following season, *Street & Smith's* magazine and Al McGuire of NBC were among those to rank the Boilermakers No. 1 in the country. The first Associated Press poll had Purdue No. 2.

After a nationally televised win at Louisville, many thought Purdue was the best team in the country. After all, they were 17-1 and in the midst of tying the longest winning streak in school history (16) and were ranked second (behind Temple) in the polls. Indiana snapped Purdue's winning streak the following week (82-79), but the Boilermakers got revenge on their archrival.

Prior to the rematch with the Hoosiers, Keady allowed CBS's cameras inside Purdue's locker room for the Boilermaker boss's pregame talk. Mitchell took Keady's words to heart, as he was sensational against IU, scoring 21 of his 24 points in the second half. His 360-degree slam dunk at the buzzer, which gave Purdue a 95-85 victory, was one of the most memorable moments of an incredible 1987-88 season.

Hard to Say It's Over

Few, including Troy Lewis himself, can forget the way his illustrious collegiate career ended. Purdue was the No. 1 seed in the Midwest Regional and rolled through the first two rounds of the 1988 NCAA Tournament. However, the season and the Anderson, Indiana, native's Purdue career came to an abrupt end when Kansas State shocked the Boilermakers 73-70 in the Pontiac (Michigan) Silverdome. It was an extra painful loss since Purdue beat the Wildcats 101-72 earlier in the season.

In the locker room after that devastating loss, Lewis had a difficult time coming to grips with the fact that he would never don the Old Gold and Black uniform again. In fact, Lewis stayed in his No. 23 jersey for 10 hours after the game.

"After the game was the first time I had seen Coach [Gene] Keady break down," Lewis said. "It was so emotional. I couldn't believe it. I didn't take off my uniform until nine o'clock the next morning.

"I felt we had a national championship team. We weren't dominating, but when we were on we felt nobody in the country could beat us. That's the thorn in my career at Purdue. I was hurt almost more for Coach Keady than for myself. He deserved to get to the Final Four."

He's Leaving;
No, He's Staying

Opportunities come with success, and that has been the case with Coach Gene Keady.

Probably the closest he ever came to leaving West Lafayette was following the 1988-89 season. Keady's team had suffered its first losing season (15-16), and he was being heavily courted by Arizona State and was interviewed for its vacancy.

He visited the Tempe campus March 12, 1989. One day earlier, Keady's Boilermakers ended their season with a 97-66 win over Northwestern in Mackey Arena. At halftime of the game, the soldout crowd started chanting "Keady." In addition, numerous signs in the arena also implored the Boilermaker boss to stay at Purdue.

On March 13, Keady told the *Purdue Exponent*, "We're looking at maybe making a change, but right now it's strictly up in the air, so we don't know."

Keady told the *Indianapolis News* that if he did take another coaching position, it would probably be his last move.

On March 14, Keady announced that he would remain at Purdue. He called Arizona State athletic director Charles Harris to turn down the job.

Keady made his decision to stay after a meeting with Purdue president Steven C. Beering and athletics director George King. According to Keady, he still wasn't sure what he would do when the meeting started.

"Walking into the meeting I really didn't know what I was going to do, because it's the most difficult decision in my career to ever make," Keady admitted.

The site of the meeting—Hovde Hall—seemed to play a pivotal role in Keady's decision-making process.

"When I walked in and I looked out the window of the administration building and I saw the tradition and knew what the people had been saying about our program all the time—how supportive they had been—at about 11:30 I decided to coach the Boilermakers next year.

"We love it here and we want to stay."

Keady announced his decision at a press conference luncheon. When he said he was staying, many of the Purdue athletics department administrators and fans in attendance cheered and gave him a standing ovation that brought tears to Keady's eyes.

According to United Press International, Arizona State offered Keady a $300,000 annual salary. He said he probably would have taken the job had he made a decision on March 12, but thought he would make a better decision if he waited.

"I didn't want to do something that I'd be sorry for later," Keady said.

Keady has had numerous opportunities to leave Purdue for other head coaching positions, but he turned them all down.

In 1984, Keady spoke with the general manager and assistant general manager of the Indiana Pacers about coaching in Indianapolis, but talks were never that serious.

A day before the 1988 Memphis State game in the NCAA Tournament, there was a rumor circulating about Keady taking the head coaching job at Texas. After the season, he told the players he wasn't going to Austin, but during the Final Four in Kansas City the rumor got even hotter. On Thursday, a couple of days before the national semifinals, a wire story said Keady was the top choice for the Texas job. On Friday, word was that Keady had met with Texas athletic director DeLoss Dodds, a college football teammate of Keady's at Kansas State. Later that afternoon, *CNN* went as far as to report that Keady would take the Texas job and started speculating as to who his successor at Purdue would be.

In May of 1988, Keady's name was linked to the New Mexico opening. He talked with New Mexico athletic director John Koenig and almost visited the campus, but backed out.

Other schools that have wanted Keady or at least were rumored to want him during his Purdue tenure include Ohio State after Eldon Miller was fired following the 1985-86 season, Kansas State, Houston, UNLV, USC and San Diego State.

Mother Nature Strikes Back

The only Purdue home football game in recent memory that Mother Nature interrupted was September 9, 1989. The Boilermakers' 27-10 win over Miami of Ohio was delayed three times for a total of 49 minutes by lightning at Ross-Ade Stadium.

The lightning during the game injured at least one person on the east side of the stadium and drove other spectators into the concourse area during the delays, which were ordered by the referee.

The storms dumped a total of a couple of inches of rain on the Lafayette area that day.

CHAPTER 6

1990s

A Little Rogaine, Please

Years before Gene Keady ever appeared on *Late Night with David Letterman*, his hair was a source of interest for Purdue fans. A fan from Crawfordsville, Indiana, wrote Keady to say that he could see his bald spot plain as day from his seat a few rows behind the Purdue bench.

Somehow the letter was brought to the attention of a couple of Keady's cronies, head baseball coach Dave Alexander and fan Tom Rehm. Alexander and Rehm, never ones to pass up such a golden opportunity for a practical joke, decided that they would send information about hair-restoration products to Keady through campus mail using a variety of athletics department names on campus mail envelopes.

For a period of a couple weeks, Keady received ads for products like Rogaine from various "individuals." Alexander and Rehm even got bold enough to send one to Keady from President Steven Beering.

A couple of days later, Keady was on the phone with Beering after a Boilermaker victory.

"Dr. Beering, I want to thank you for sending me the information about the hair product," Keady reportedly said.

"Coming from you, I will give it some thought."

There was silence on the other end of the line.

Beering had no idea what Keady was talking about and told the coach so. It didn't take Keady much longer to connect the dots, nor to find his resident practical jokesters and *former* friends. Alexander and Rehm had a laugh that lasted them for a while, and Keady showed his good sense of humor, knowing he had been had.

Quite a Reception

A crowd estimated at 500 by the Purdue University Police Department was on hand January 13, 1990, to welcome the Boilermaker men's basketball team back from their 81-79 overtime win at No. 13 Indiana.

The generally orderly crowd chanted, sang and even climbed light poles awaiting the team's arrival.

Once the team bus arrived about 1:30 a.m. on January 14, the fans flocked to it, impeding its progress down North University Drive. Some fans even climbed to the top of the bus. When the players finally disembarked, the crowd cheered loudly. It had chants of praise for junior forward Chuckie White, who had 19 points in the win. They screamed, "Chuckie! Chuckie!"

"I remember people were jumping all over the bus," center Stephen Scheffler said. "Cornelius McNary was afraid to get off the bus. That was fun."

The gathering also touched Coach Gene Keady.

"It was a fabulous feeling, because you don't get that very often," Keady said. "The timing of it made it special because of who we beat.

"The students have always been a special part of our program."

Some fans even pounded on the windows of the coaches' offices once the players and coaches went inside Mackey Arena.

Highway Robbery

Coach Gene Keady's fourth Big Ten title came in 1994, but it could have come in 1990, as his team had one literally stolen from it.

One of the lowlights of Stephen Scheffler's career was a 72-70 loss March 11, 1990, at Michigan State's brand-new Breslin Center. That defeat in the regular-season finale cost Purdue a share of the Big Ten title.

The Boilermakers didn't it make it to East Lansing until the early morning hours due to foggy conditions that forced them to land in Detroit and bus the rest of the way. But what happened to them on the court caused many a sleepless night among Boilermaker faithful.

"I remember toward the end of the game we led and had to get the ball inbounds," recalled Scheffler. "Just before that, they called timeout and were going to intentionally foul. One of their players was grabbing Tony Jones's shirt, yanking it like you would a football player's, and I couldn't believe they didn't call a foul. We couldn't get the ball in so we had to call timeout.

"We ran the play, I grabbed the ball and was thinking, 'Get the ball to Tony.' I don't remember how, but they ended up stealing the ball from me. I remember watching the game film and saying, 'Wow, I really got fouled.' I should have just held on to the ball, taken the foul and went to the line."

I'm Mad as Hell and I'm Not Going to Take It Any More

Coach Gene Keady couldn't hold back his feelings following a 73-72 loss to Texas in the second round of the 1990 NCAA Tournament before 37,842 fans in Indianapolis's Hoosier Dome.

At the press conference following the game, Keady exploded. When the NCAA moderator asked Keady to make an opening statement, at first the Boilermaker boss said he didn't have much to say, then he let the refs have it.

"It's heartbreaking; that's what you call it when … you can't get calls from the officials," Keady said. "That's all bull——.

"There were three charges they didn't call; that's ridiculous. You have the same thing happen at Michigan State [one week earlier in a 72-70 loss in East Lansing that cost the Boilermakers a share of the Big Ten championship].

"You run a program and you graduate all your kids, you don't cheat, you do things right and," Keady then slammed the press table, "the God;—— referees are all the same.

"I get tired of it. I've got good kids who work hard and they're in there crying their eyes out because we've got some guys who don't understand the game."

Keady's outburst cost him dearly. He was fined $10,000 by the NCAA.

The Boilermakers would have been victorious had it not been for a blocked shot by Texas's Panama Myers in the final seconds. On a set play, guard Tony Jones drove the length of the floor and appeared to have an open lane for a layup and the win. Myers (6'8") slid off his man and blocked Jones's shot before it hit the backboard and held onto the ball as time expired.

Purdue also was hurt when center Stephen Scheffler suffered his worst shooting night as a Boilermaker. He hit just six of 17 shots from the field after leading the country in field-goal shooting during the regular season.

Doubting His Ability

By the time he was a senior in 1989-90, Stephen Scheffler was one of college basketball's most intimidating and effective centers.

Despite starting just one game in his first two seasons in West Lafayette, Scheffler was a force that few opponents had an answer for during his junior and senior seasons.

The six-foot-nine, 240-pound center from Ada, Michigan, averaged 14.9 points and 6.1 rebounds per game while shooting 68.3 percent from the floor (319 of 467) and 79.3 percent from the free throw line (268 of 338) in his final two seasons at Purdue (1988-89 and 1989-90).

Surprisingly Scheffler, whose physical style of play rivaled any other player at the time as he occasionally wore football thigh pads under his playing shorts, questioned his basketball ability early in his Purdue career.

"His freshman year he went through the same frustrations that Brian [Cardinal] went through," recalled former assistant coach Bruce Weber. "Asking himself, 'Do I belong? Maybe I should have played football.'"

Scheffler exited Forest Hills Northern High School as an All-State center and was the football team's Most Valuable Player and an All-State defensive tackle his senior year.

At that time, he was considered a much better football prospect than basketball, and the likes of Michigan's Bo Schembechler offered him a scholarship.

"I think Michigan wanted me to play either offensive or defensive tackle," said Scheffler, who took an official visit to Michigan.

"I think during my freshman year at Purdue, the [basketball] coaches were hoping that I would switch to football so I would free up a scholarship. [Purdue assistant coach] Dave Wood told me when I was a junior, 'Steve, when you came in here we looked at you, and you were our biggest recruiting mistake.'"

Early in his collegiate career, Scheffler said he thought about playing football at Purdue.

"The nice thing about football is you don't have to worry about fouls," Scheffler explained. "You just go against guys and nail them.

"What helped me confirm my situation was I had a summer class with some football players and they were all wearing shorts. I told them, 'You guys all have the same tattoos,' because they all had the same scars across their knees. I asked them, 'How many of you have not had shoulder or knee surgery?' They said, 'The punter hasn't.' Then I thought that wasn't for me, especially when you consider you can work so hard, for so long and then have it all blown away [with an injury]."

Scheffler often inflicted pain on the opposition on the hardwood. When he wasn't scoring or pulling down a key rebound, he was setting devastating screens to free up Troy Lewis and Company.

"I definitely wasn't a finesse player," Scheffler said. "My freshman and sophomore years, my whole goal was to get Troy Lewis open. I literally tried to set a back pick and try to hit the guy so hard or he would hit into me so hard that he would fall to the ground. Then I thought I did something good. I didn't want my guy to score or get a rebound and I wanted to get Troy Lewis open.

"My game was ugly, but creatively effective."

It was so effective that he earned 1990 Big Ten Player of the Year honors and was named third-team All-American. In addition, he broke a 28-year-old conference single-season shooting percentage mark (.767 in 1990 league games only) and finished 19th on the school's all-time scoring list (1,155 points).

Scheffler set the NCAA career field goal percentage record (.685) and ranked second in the country in shooting accuracy in 1989-90 (.698).

In his four years, Purdue won 73.4 percent of its games (91-33), including 72.2 percent of its Big Ten contests (52-20).

Not bad for someone who didn't think he belonged as a college basketball player.

Mackey Arena Becomes Mr. Robinson's Neighborhood

Luring Glenn Robinson to Purdue was arguably the greatest recruiting catch ever in the school's history.

The Gary (Indiana) Roosevelt High School standout was considered the nation's best high school player (along with Michigan's Chris Webber) by recruiting analyst Bob Gibbons.

Robinson decided that Purdue was the place for him after visiting the West Lafayette campus the weekend of October 20, 1990. He officially announced his decision November 1, 1990, at a press conference held in the Roosevelt gym.

Purdue was the first school to recruit Robinson and even had him attend its summer basketball camp. By the time he was a sophomore, Coach Gene Keady and assistant coach Frank Kendrick had made Robinson well aware that he was their prized recruit in the class of 1991.

"Coach [Keady] called him and said, 'You can play whatever position you want to play,'" said Cuonzo Martin, who also signed with Purdue in 1990-91, but went to prep school that season and later became Robinson's closest friend and roommate at Purdue. "The fortunate thing for Purdue was that he was a local kid.

"A lot of people from the Gary area and Roosevelt High School went to Purdue, so I think a lot of those people worked Glenn and talked to him about coming to Purdue. That helped a lot.

"Everyone on the 'Fab Five' was calling him trying to get him to go to Michigan."

When Robinson announced his intentions to attend Purdue, he said, "I just felt like it was time. I feel comfortable with Purdue."

Robinson had planned to make official visits to Tennessee, UNLV and Syracuse, but cancelled them after his weekend in West Lafayette. Michigan, which signed the "Fab Five" that year, made a serious pitch for Robinson's services, but it fell on deaf ears.

After Purdue played one of its preseason Black and Gold scrimmages at Roosevelt in the fall of 1990, Roosevelt coach Ron Heflin said Robinson had two plane tickets on the coach's desk to go to UNLV—a national power at the time. Robinson, however, told Heflin to call Runnin' Rebels coach Jerry Tarkanian to tell him he wasn't going to visit Vegas and that he had made up his mind.

Indiana's Bob Knight wanted Robinson so badly that he sent

Glenn Robinson

assistant coach Joby Wright up to Roosevelt High School, but Robinson wouldn't even talk to the IU assistant.

Robinson lived up to his billing, as he went on to lead the nation in scoring in 1993-94 and was the consensus 1994 National Player of the Year.

Supreme Court Defector

For quite a while, Purdue looked to be in great shape to land Indianapolis Brebeuf standout Alan Henderson in the fall of 1990. Henderson would have joined Glenn Robinson and Brandon Brantley in what would have been the nation's second best recruiting class behind Michigan's "Fab Five."

Robinson, Henderson and Brantley were featured on the cover of *Gold & Black Illustrated* and dubbed "The Supreme Court," as the trio took part in a photo shoot inside and outside the Lafayette Courthouse.

Brantley verbally committed to Purdue in late September, and Robinson gave his pledge to Coach Gene Keady and Co. in October. That left all eyes focused on Henderson. If he opted for Purdue, the trio would form the best frontcourt Purdue had ever signed in one year and possibly the best recruiting class in school history.

Like Robinson, the six-foot-nine Henderson was rated among the top 10 players in the country. He visited Stanford and Indiana and had official trips to Duke, Northwestern and Purdue scheduled.

The Boilermaker coaching staff was encouraged by what they were hearing privately. Henderson said he would take all of his visits and then announce a decision if he felt ready. Purdue would be the last school Henderson visited.

Shortly after Robinson committed, he telephoned Henderson to tell him of his choice before he went public with it. The two were the main contenders for Indiana's prestigious Mr. Basketball Award in 1991.

Henderson, projected as a small forward, said he wouldn't at all mind playing with Robinson, a power forward.

"You always have to look at what players are in a program," Henderson said at the time. "The better the players, the more success you can have. Glenn going to Purdue will be a plus for Purdue. I want to play with great players.

"We've talked about going to the same place, and I would say it would influence my decision knowing where he was going.

I think he'd like to play with me, and I know I wouldn't mind being on the same team with him."

Unfortunately for Boilermaker fans, Henderson and Robinson ended up facing one another rather than playing on the same team. Henderson decided that Indiana was the place for him.

Henderson said he found no faults with Purdue or its basketball program; it was simply a matter of having a gut feeling for IU.

"It wasn't anything they [the Boilermakers] didn't have or that turned me off," Henderson said. "It was just the feeling that Indiana was the place for me."

Just how lethal would Purdue have been with Robinson and Henderson in the frontcourt?

"Glenn Robinson and Alan Henderson on the same team would've been tougher to guard than Chris Webber and Juwan Howard, but it didn't work out," Boilermaker forward Cuonzo Martin said.

"What About the Assistant Coaches?"

There were some fireworks during Fred Akers's press conference to announce his resignation as Purdue's football head coach November 29, 1990.

As Purdue athletics director George King cited the reasons for Akers's departure, defensive coordinator Phil Bennett, watching the conference on television from his home, became irate when King talked about the outstanding groups of coaches available to fill the vacancies, making specific mention of the LSU staff.

Bennett stormed into the VIP Room in Mackey Arena, where

the press conference was being held, and confronted King as he was fielding the media's questions. Bennett said there were still some excellent assistants at Purdue. King calmly acknowledged Bennett and said Akers's assistants all would have the opportunity to interview to be on the new coach's staff.

In an ironic twist, Bennett was named linebackers coach at LSU under new Tiger boss Curley Hallman a few days later. King reportedly respected Bennett for standing up for himself when the two met later in King's office.

EEE-jected!

The only time Gene Keady has been ejected from a Purdue game was March 2, 1991, at Iowa. Keady was called for two technical fouls, and assistant coach Bruce Weber had to act as the Boilermakers' head coach.

"I got kicked out and we won," Keady recalled. "We came back from 16 down. The people were great to me in the back [recesses of Carver-Hawkeye Arena]. They were giving me pizza and Coke when we were behind. When we got ahead, they just left me. No, I'm just kidding … they were fine."

Purdue ended up winning the game 70-65, which went a long way in helping the Boilermakers make the 1991 NCAA Tournament.

"Magnet from Mansfield"

Joy Holmes came to Purdue in the fall of 1987 from Mansfield, Ohio, as a rather unpublicized recruit. But after averaging merely 4.8 points and 2.3 rebounds during her freshman year, she went on to become one of the greatest women's basketball players in school history.

Blessed with good speed and quick hands, Holmes was nicknamed the "Magnet from Mansfield" because of her propensity for steals. She shattered the school season record with 100 steals in 1988-89 and followed it up with back-to-back 99-steal campaigns. (Her record ultimately was broken by Katie Douglas with 101 in 2000-01 and then by Kelly Komara with 120 in 2001-02.)

As a senior in 1990-91, Holmes was named Purdue's first-ever Big Ten Player of the Year and Kodak All-American after averaging 21.5 points and 9.2 rebounds per game. She led the conference in rebounds and steals while ranking second in blocked shots, third in scoring, fifth in field goal percentage and eighth in free throw percentage.

Her career total of 323 steals stood for 10 years until Douglas amassed 327 from 1998 to 2001, although Douglas played in 15 more games. In fact, Douglas broke the mark in her final game with six swipes in the NCAA title game against Notre Dame on April 1, 2001.

Holmes still holds the school record with 12 steals in a game (tied for the most in Big Ten history) against Minnesota on January 13, 1989.

Victory Garden

Prior to the 1991 season, Coach Jim Colletto had a mock cemetery, about 30 feet wide and 50 feet long, named "Victory Garden" built adjacent to the Mollenkopf Athletic Center, complete with a white picket fence.

A gravestone was placed inside the cemetery for each Purdue road victory and for any upset win.

Colletto got the idea for the Victory Garden from the Florida State coaching staff when he was an assistant at Arizona State in the mid-1980s. Florida State coaches claimed part of their team's success was attributed to the pride the players felt with each addition to their Victory Garden.

"This seemed like a neat opportunity to do it here," Colletto said. "I think the players will get a big kick out of it when they get to put a stone in there."

The first stone came following the Boilermakers' 1991 win at Northwestern. The second stone came after the 1992 upset over California.

After the Cal game, Colletto entered the postgame press conference carrying the headstone, and he told the media that someone had placed it in his office sometime during the week prior to the game.

The Boilermakers paid their final respects in a memorial ceremony for their fallen foe two days after the game. In addition to the date and the final score of the Cal game being on the tombstone, the inscription on it read, "Correct the past. Rule the present. See to the future."

When all was said and done, the Victory Garden had eight tombstones in it. The last one came following Purdue's 9-3 upset over No. 9 Michigan on November 9, 1996, just a few days after Colletto had resigned.

In the spring of 1997, Coach Joe Tiller announced that the Victory Garden would be a thing of the past.

"I don't like it," he said. "We want to place more emphasis on being consistent in what we're doing. In other words, we want to raise the expectation level. I think the problem with that is that it allows you to have a lower expectation level, so when you do something it becomes a big deal instead of an ordinary task.

"I thought it was a good idea if it involved huge, significant wins. To me, a huge, significant win is against a huge, significant opponent … a win against a top 10 team."

Short Day's Work

Women's basketball player Jane Calhoun was known for aggressive play and all-out effort during her career from 1987 to 1992. Sometimes it got her into trouble with the officials, like on the afternoon of December 29, 1991. Purdue was playing Loyola-Chicago in the championship game of the Boilermaker Classic, and Calhoun fouled out in *four* minutes. She also scored four points and pulled down a rebound in the short day's work.

Calhoun's collegiate career got off to a short start, too, as she suffered a broken right foot just five minutes into her first game against Eastern Illinois on November 28, 1987. But after redshirting that season, Calhoun came back to be a dependable player for the Boilermakers, capped by her being named to the program's All-Decade team in 1992.

Double-Duty Donna

Three-fourths of the way through her collegiate basketball career, Donna Gill decided she wanted to play volleyball, as well.

So, in the fall of 1991, Gill joined the volleyball team and immediately became a starting middle blocker. On November 22, she set a school record with 16 blocks against Michigan at home, then woke up the next morning and flew to Bowling Green, Ohio, where the women's basketball team was opening its season. For the season, Gill led the volleyball team in hitting percentage (.247) and blocks (1.45, third most in Purdue history), then topped the women's basketball team in rebounds (7.4) and ranked second in scoring (11.2) en route to being named second-team All-Big Ten.

In 1992, with her basketball eligibility expired, Gill was able to concentrate solely on volleyball and earned honorable mention All-Conference laurels after again pacing Purdue in hitting percentage (.335, sixth highest in school history) and blocks (1.53, second most in school annals). Along the way, she tied her own match record with 16 blocks against Indiana on October 21.

Following her collegiate days, Gill moved to Fairbanks, Alaska, where she met Bev Krupa and had an influence on her coming to Purdue to play volleyball from 1995 to 1998.

Spoiling IU's Big Ten Title Hopes

When Purdue fans stormed the Mackey Arena court to celebrate a 61-59 victory over No. 4 Indiana on March 15, 1992, it marked the first and only time fans had celebrated a victory by being on the court in Mackey Arena history.

Purdue's stunning win denied IU a share of the Big Ten title and a top seed in the NCAA Tournament. It allowed Ohio State to win the Big Ten championship outright, prompting Columbus mayor Greg Lashutka to declare March 15 as "Purdue Day" in the Buckeye capital city.

Several minutes after the game concluded, Purdue students could still be heard yelling and screaming on the floor as the press conference was going on.

Indiana coach Bob Knight, looking dazed, made a brief appearance in the postgame press conference, just long enough to see Purdue guard Woody Austin at the podium before doing an about-face and vanishing to the team bus.

The win erased Purdue's memories of its worst defeat to IU in series history. The Hoosiers had beaten the Boilermakers 106-65 just six weeks earlier in Assembly Hall.

In the rematch, IU led 42-32 with 12:31 left, when Austin took over, putting on one of the greatest displays of basketball in Mackey history over the next four minutes.

Purdue went on a 15-3 run to reclaim the lead at 47-45. During the rally, Austin was unstoppable. He scored the final 10 points of the run over a span of 3:35. He finished the game with 20 points on eight-of-20 shooting, hitting all six of his shots in the second half.

After the game, senior center Craig Riley, who had 15 points, said, "This makes my whole career worthwhile. You dream about this when you're nine years old. To come in here, win a game and ruin their championship hopes means everything. You can't top it. It's bragging rights for the rest of my life."

Knight never has been a good loser and showed his true colors the following season. When his Indiana team visited Mackey the following year, Knight had Indiana's media relations office issue a statement that said, "Due to the fact Indiana players have class tomorrow and that the Hoosiers must bus back to Bloomington (per Big Ten rules) after the game, there will be no press conference with Indiana coach Bob Knight or Indiana players.

"After Indiana's game here last year, Knight waited over 30 minutes to appear in the press room, and when he arrived, Purdue players were still at the podium. By leaving as soon as possible following tonight's game, this will allow IU players to get back and be able to go to class tomorrow and eliminate any problems which happened last year."

Knight, however, did let Calbert Cheancy do a postgame interview with ESPN color analyst Dick Vitale, recognized by many in college basketball circles as a Knight worshipper.

Recruiting Wars: The Tough Losses

Coach Gene Keady has pretty much seen and heard it all during his time in West Lafayette, particularly when it comes to recruiting.

Following are some recruiting tidbits that have transpired through the Keady years.

Jerome Harmon was a heralded player out of Gary Wallace High School who had sensational leaping ability. He had narrowed his choices to Purdue and Louisville. Back when coaches could comment on recruits prior to them signing their national letters of intent, Keady said, "If we ever get him, we're going to run his butt off," referring to how many man hours, particularly by assistant coach Bruce Weber, had been put into recruiting him. As it turned out, Harmon ended up signing with Louisville. One of his reasons, among others, was that he was concerned that Purdue had some racial problems on its campus.

Rick Fox of Warsaw, Indiana, had narrowed his choices down to Purdue and North Carolina. Fox's high school coach, Al Rhodes, called Keady in his office to inform the Boilermaker boss that his star player would be headed to Tobacco Road. After the brief conversation, Keady slammed the phone, fired off a few expletives, and continued conducting an interview with the *Purdue Exponent.*

Purdue coaches began recruiting Eric Anderson when he was a freshman in his Chicago-area high school and didn't stop until he announced for Indiana in the fall signing period of his senior year.

"We basically recruited him straight through," Weber said. "We saw him his sophomore and junior years seven or eight times, at least, and in the camps we saw him every day for a couple of weeks. You saw a kid like that 30 or 40 times."

Recruiting Wars Part II: The Victories

Conversely, Purdue spent little time recruiting Jimmy Oliver, Arkansas's Mr. Basketball. He played his high school career in near-seclusion in Menifee, Arkansas. The Boilermakers signed Oliver in the spring, a last-minute catch that worked out well.

"We were able to recruit Jimmy from talking to a coach from another school in Texas," Purdue assistant Bruce Weber said. "He said, 'There's a kid in Arkansas you might want to look at.' He [Oliver] was going JUCO [junior college] the whole way. Schools like Arkansas and Houston had seen him, but his coach thought he should go to a JUCO. Then we got involved. I went down and talked about our academics and about getting out of Arkansas. They trusted Coach [Keady] and they thought it would be good. That was a luck thing.

"That's the thing about it. Eric Anderson you see 40 times, Jimmy Oliver you see once. Some kids you call every week, some kids you call three times. And the kid you call three times ends up better a lot of times."

Another player Purdue worked long and hard to sign was Antoine Joubert, the standout guard from Detroit who went to Michigan. If the Boilermakers had landed Joubert, they probably would not have been able to get Troy Lewis the following year—a fact Lewis confirmed—because Lewis played the same position as Joubert.

Lewis's classmate, Todd Mitchell, was involved in an interesting recruiting story. He enjoyed a shopping spree on a visit he made to Minnesota. Mitchell was taken to a sporting goods store owned by Gopher coach Jim Dutcher and was permitted to buy items at tremendously discounted prices, like $5 for a pair of new shoes.

Kip Jones was a blue-chip recruit who played in the Dapper Dan All-Star Game the summer prior to his senior year at Bellmont High School in Decatur, Indiana. He asked Weber how much he would get paid if he came to Purdue. One of the players Jones met at the All-Star Game, who was headed to a Big East school, said he was going to make $200 a month. Weber told him "nothing" and Jones came to Purdue anyway.

Purdue's "M.J."

In basketball circles around the country, "M.J." almost always is used in reference to NBA great Michael Jordan. But in West Lafayette in the late 1980s and early '90s, "M.J." stood for MaChelle Joseph, the all-time leading scorer in Purdue basketball history.

Joseph scored 2,405 points (20.2 per game) from 1989 to 1992. By comparison, the all-time leading men's scorer, Rick Mount, had 2,323 points, albeit without the benefit of the three-point shot and completing the task in three varsity seasons. Joseph was a model of consistency, averaging 18.9 points as a freshman, 19.4 as a sophomore, 20.3 as a junior and a school-record 22.2 as a senior. Her senior year, she was named the Big Ten Player of the Year, Big Ten Female Athlete of the Year and a Kodak All-American.

Following her playing days, Joseph served as an assistant coach at Illinois in 1992-93 before returning to Purdue as an assistant from 1994 to 1996, helping the Boilermakers reach the 1994 NCAA Women's Final Four. She more or less fell off the Purdue landscape when head coach Lin Dunn was fired in 1996. Despite her accomplishments as a player and a coach, Joseph has yet to be inducted into the Purdue Intercollegiate Athletics Hall of Fame.

He Aimed High and Got It

In the United States Air Force, wrestler Charles Jones learned to "Aim High." He carried that slogan over to the mat and achieved the pinnacle in collegiate wrestling.

Jones, who spent six years as a sergeant in the Air Force (1982-88), became the first Purdue wrestler in more than 40 years to win an NCAA championship on March 21, 1992, in Oklahoma City.

Jones, a senior from Sandusky, Ohio, defeated Todd Chesbro of Oklahoma State 6-5 to win the 167-pound weight class. Jones was the No. 2 seed heading into the NCAA's.

"Being the national champion is wonderful," Jones said at

the time. "It's a great honor because it has been quite a while since anyone has done it, and it gets recognition for the school."

Six days prior to the weigh-in for the championships, Jones was 20 pounds overweight. He was able to cut weight by sitting in a sauna wearing a plastic sweatsuit. He said he lost approximately seven pounds in an hour. His normal weight ranged from the upper 180s to lower 190s, while his body fat hovered around five percent.

In two years at Purdue, Jones compiled a 65-5 record, including 31-1 as a senior. He finished third at the NCAA championship in 1991. Jones was a Big Ten champion in 1992 and runner-up in 1991.

Jones joined Arnold Plaza as one of two Boilermaker wrestlers to win an NCAA individual championship since 1950.

Miracle Comeback

No Purdue player ever has defied the odds more than Darryl Stingley.

The former Boilermaker and New England Patriot wide receiver became a quadriplegic August 12, 1978, after taking a vicious hit from Oakland Raiders defensive back Jack Tatum during a preseason game.

Stingley ran a slant pattern over the middle—a play called 94 Slant to be exact. New England quarterback Steve Grogan's pass was high, and in an attempt to haul it in, Stingley elevated. It was out of his reach, and as he was coming down, Tatum delivered a devastating blow, which many believed to be a cheap shot.

To this day, Tatum, who played at Ohio State from 1970 to 1972, never has offered an apology to Stingley, who broke his neck, severing his fourth and fifth vertebrae, on the play.

Nearly 14 years after that hit, Stingley returned to Purdue to participate in graduation ceremonies May 9, 1992, after earning his bachelor's degree in physical education.

With his mother, Hilda, by his side, Stingley received his

diploma and received a standing ovation from the Elliott Hall of Music crowd of 6,027 at the annual commencement exercises.

As Stingley was presented with his degree, Purdue president Steven Beering echoed the sentiments of thousands of admirers when he said, "Darryl Stingley, we salute your courage. You're an example and inspiration to all of us."

The news of Stingley's graduation was reported nationwide. The *New York Times* covered the event, while CNN, the *CBS Evening News* and *Entertainment Tonight* aired related stories. *USA Today*, *Sports Illustrated* and the *Chicago Tribune* ran stories in the weeks preceding the event.

Stingley, who wore No. 43 at Purdue, overcame incredible odds to earn his degree as well as survive such a severe injury.

He completed his degree requirements through correspondence courses at City-wide College of Chicago. He took courses by way of cable television, following lesson plans provided by the school. Purdue accepted the work, which took Stingley two years to complete.

"My only problem was my disability," said Stingley of earning his degree. "It wouldn't allow me to jot down certain things or make special notations, so I have my wife [Martine] to thank for being instrumental and going through this whole thing with me. She was there every step of the way. I can't say enough about the sacrifices she made so I could get it done."

The 1968 Chicago High School Player of the Year was an All-Big Ten pick at Purdue.

Now in his fifties, Stingley continues to have a limited range of motion in his right arm, which he has had since the injury, and he can feel his left arm but cannot move it. He and his wife live in downtown Chicago along the lakefront in a custom-built condominium, which cost about $1 million. There is a lot of voice-activated technology throughout their home.

"As we speak, I'm a relatively healthy person," said Stingley, who weighs about 200 pounds, just 10 pounds more than he did when he was playing at Purdue. "I'm as good as I can be.

"Yes, I lost a lot physically, but through all of that I gained a lot more spiritually. I live, breathe and have command of all my senses. I'm just as alive as anybody else. This tragic accident has incapacitated me in a major form, but it hasn't been something that has actually stopped me from pursuing what I wanted to do."

He now helps Chicago's inner-city youth through the Darryl Stingley Foundation, Inc.

"I've been blessed to be in this situation. I just really can't complain," he said.

Hello "$$$"

When Mitch Hull resigned as wrestling coach on May 26, 1992, he submitted his letter to the Lafayette *Journal and Courier*, which ran it verbatim. Hull argued that in addition to him being the lowest-paid wrestling coach in the Big Ten, many other athletics department employees were underpaid.

So in its next-day edition, the *Journal and Courier* published a list of salaries of every coach, administrator and employee in the department. Needless to say, it raised some eyebrows. And for the next couple of days, virtually everyone called each other by his or her salary as opposed to their name.

Of the 67 individuals who had their salaries listed, only 19 were with the department as of July 1, 2003 (28 percent), including two who left and returned.

29-Cent Investment

Upon returning from a business trip to Minnesota for Inland Steel Co. the Friday of Memorial Day weekend in 1992, Morgan Burke's wife, Kate, mentioned that she had read in the *Chicago Tribune* that George King Jr. was retiring as Purdue's athletics director. Morgan and George's son, George III, were fraternity brothers at Purdue, and Morgan knew the entire King family from his days as a lifeguard at the Lafayette Country Club.

So, soon after hearing of King's retirement plans, Morgan decided to call George Jr. to wish him well. "We had been talking awhile, and George said to me, 'You've got the background they're looking for,' Morgan recalls. 'If I were you, I'd invest 29 cents on a stamp and put your resume in the mail.' I told Kate, and we chuckled about it. It was the furthest thing in our minds. Then a few days later, she came back to me and said, 'You would really like that job.' So I decided to throw my name in the ring. I've been told that I was always in the third pile, which I don't think is the good pile to be in, but they kept coming back to me."

Burke ultimately was hired in November of 1992 and assumed the duties as Purdue's 11th athletics director on New Year's Day of 1993.

Pennies ... Well, Dollars from Heaven

Morgan Burke had just come to Purdue as an athletics director full of big plans and ideas. Admittedly, it took Burke some time to get used to his new position and his staff to get used to him.

Burke was an attorney who had left a position at Inland Steel for the new job in West Lafayette. There were some on the staff who questioned his ability to relate to coaches. Burke's athletic career at Purdue was substantial, as he captained the swimming team as a senior in 1972-73. Still, some wondered how well a swimmer could administrate big-time sports like football and men's basketball.

When Burke took over, the football program was in the depths of depression and money was hard to come by for much-needed projects. Burke got a big break when Howard "Monk" Kissell donated $750,000 to finish off the Mollenkopf Athletic Center in a gift that seemingly came from heaven. Kissell played on the Boilermakers' lone undisputed Big Ten football championship team in 1929.

"That one generous act proved to me and others that big things like this could happen at Purdue," Burke said. "It truly was a turning point and helped us move forward with the golf course, aquatics center and stadium renovation. Without Monk taking the lead, who knows what would have happened."

Under Burke's watch, Purdue athletics have enjoyed their greatest fundraising and facilities growth in the history of the school.

Upset and Upsetting

The football team played arguably its finest game in the six-year tenure of Jim Colletto against visiting California on September 12, 1992. The Boilermakers blitzed the 17th-ranked Golden Bears 41-14 and were recognized by the *Chicago Tribune* for posting the "Upset of the Week."

During his weekly press conference the following Tuesday, Colletto warned about bringing his team back down to earth in preparation for its next game against Toledo, a squad far inferior to Cal. "I don't want to be the 'Upset of the Week' two weeks in a row," he said, knowing the Boilermakers were heavy favorites.

Sure enough, in a game on which the Associated Press didn't even offer a spread because the Boilermakers were such heavy favorites, Toledo stunned Purdue 33-29.

In the loss, freshman fullback Mike Alstott scored the first of his school-record 42 touchdowns on a six-yard pass from Matt Pike in the third quarter.

Taking Offense to Hicks Stereotype

The day before the Purdue-California game on September 12, 1992, some of the Golden Bears players showed up for practice in Ross-Ade Stadium wearing cowboy hats and chewing on straw, poking fun at the Midwest and Purdue.

The Golden Bears were convinced that the Midwestern farm boys from Purdue would be no match.

Purdue quarterback Matt Pike and defensive tackle Eric Gray observed the arrogance as the Bears got off their team bus.

Cal's flippant attitude carried into the opening kickoff, and they paid dearly, being whipped from start to finish 41-14.

Word of the Bears' taunting spread through the Boilermaker camp quickly, and before the game Coach Jim Colletto told his squad that Cal expected to embarrass the Boilermakers.

Defensive tackle Jeff Zgonina said the players got the message, so much so that the Boilermakers rolled to a 38-3 halftime lead over the 17th-ranked team in the country.

"Maybe now they'll go home in their cowboy hats and pieces of straw hanging out of their mouths and think a little more of the Midwest," Colletto said. "I'm not too fond of the Berkeley Bears. I'm glad they have a long trip home.

"I don't think they respected us coming in. I don't know if the coaches didn't respect us, but I don't think their players did."

Zgonina added, "I hope they got nice hats to wear. I don't think they'll be wearing them any more. I doubt their coach will ever let them wear those hats ever again."

The story, however, took an interesting turn three days following the game. Cal athletic director Bob Bockrath, a former assistant coach at Purdue, issued a statement that said, "There have been various news accounts of an alleged incident of our players wearing straw hats and chewing on stalks of grass. We investigated and found absolutely no evidence at all. It clearly was a fabrication used as a motivational tool by Purdue's coaching staff."

In 1991, Cal was nicknamed the "Bad Mouth Bears" by Pac-10 foes for trash-talking on the field.

Purdue interim athletics director John Hicks sent a letter to Bockrath saying a "great deal of exaggeration" was involved in the story, and he apologized for the entire ordeal. Colletto, however, insisted the incident happened, but perhaps to a lesser degree than originally believed.

"I heard about it two or three times," Colletto said. "I made mention of it to the team [the night before the game], but it kind of got out of hand."

Rashard Should Have Been a Boilermaker

I f there was one recruit who could have delivered Coach Gene Keady a national championship or at least a berth in the Final Four, it was Chicago's Rashard Griffith.

Griffith was a seven-foot-one, 260-pound stud from legendary hoops powerhouse Chicago Martin Luther King High School. He was a candidate for national High School Player of the Year honors and was considered the premier big man in the country. The *Chicago Tribune* called Griffith, "the most sought-after basketball talent ever to come out of the Chicago area."

Purdue had good reason to believe it would lure Griffith. He and Boilermaker Glenn Robinson had developed a good friendship playing in a college/pro league at the Malcolm X Gymnasium in Chicago during the summers of 1991 and 1992.

"He [Robinson] said if I come down there, we can win a couple of national championships, and they can help us by giving us the national attention we want," Griffith told *Gold & Black Illustrated.* "The NBA scouts will come in and evaluate us and hopefully we'll accomplish our dream."

After unofficially visiting Purdue in September, Griffith

took his official visit to Purdue the weekend of October 30 to November 1, 1992, and sat on the bench for "Midnight Magic." He was extremely impressed by the standing-room-only crowd in excess of 14,123.

The overflow crowd, which was the audience for the first official practice for the 1992-93 Boilermakers, chanted, "We want Rashard." There were signs and banners all over campus.

During his official visit, he said that his decision would likely come down to Purdue and Wisconsin, as Arizona and Oklahoma had made a late pitch for his services.

A few days after visiting Purdue, Griffith verbally committed to Wisconsin, a program that hadn't won a Big Ten championship since 1947.

"In my four years at Purdue, there were two guys that we as a team worked harder to get and that was Rashard Griffith and Roy Hairston," former player and current assistant coach Cuonzo Martin said. "We worked Rashard. We followed him everywhere on his visit. We went out at night just to do everything to get this guy because we knew we had him. He and Glenn were friends and they hung out a lot in the summer so we just knew he was coming to Purdue.

"I'll never forget that we started practicing the day he was going home and he told the team, 'I'm coming to Purdue.' That whole weekend he said, 'I'm coming to Purdue. This is the place for me.' We were excited about that. The next day I think he committed to Wisconsin. It was a tough blow for us. He was definitely the piece we needed to win the national title."

According to his mother, Elaine, who was heavily involved in the recruiting process of her son, Rashard chose Wisconsin because he wanted to play for Coach Stu Jackson. She said her favorite was Purdue. In fact, Griffith canceled a recruiting visit to Ohio State because he supposedly had the flu. However, it was later discovered that he spent the weekend playing basketball with Robinson.

"Purdue was very nice," Griffith's mother said. "That would have been my choice, but it wasn't his."

Later during the 1992-93 season, Griffith attended Purdue's

game at Northwestern. After the Boilermaker victory, he approached Robinson to talk, but the "Big Dog" wanted nothing to do with him and did a 180 as soon as he saw him and walked away.

"I think Glenn felt like Rashard's decision was a slap in the face," Martin said, "because he felt like they were good friends and Rashard told him he was coming to Purdue. I think Glenn felt like he lied to him and mistreated him. He was upset about it, but he said, 'I'll get him when we play him.'"

As it turned out, Griffith only played one season for Jackson, who left Wisconsin for the NBA.

It was little consolation for Purdue that more than three years later Griffith would admit he made the wrong choice.

In the March 14, 1995, edition of the Oshkosh (Wisconsin) *Northwestern*, Griffith said he regretted not choosing Purdue over Wisconsin.

Griffith, who led the Big Ten in rebounding and blocked shots in 1994-95, said he and Robinson might have been able to lead the Boilermakers to the national championship.

Griffith, while watching Purdue defeat Michigan 73-67 on March 12, 1995, in the regular-season finale, told the newspaper, "I have regrets that I didn't go [to Purdue]. I've said, 'Man, if I went there last year we could have won the national championship, plain and simple.'"

A case in point for the difference Griffith could have made is that Purdue's starting center, Brandon Brantley, failed to score a point and grabbed just nine rebounds in four games in the 1994 NCAA Tournament.

And Yummy Makes Three

Lin Dunn earned the reputation of being a tireless recruiter during her nine years in West Lafayette. She also was willing to do whatever it took—within the rules—to land a player she wanted.

Consider Danielle McCulley's official visit during the fall of 1992. The forward from Gary, Indiana, was accompanied to Purdue by her mother, grandmother and her grandmother's pet *pig*, named Yummy. Knowing full well that Yummy would not be welcome at the Purdue Memorial Union, Dunn agreed to lodge the pig at her apartment. So Yummy spent the weekend in Dunn's bathtub.

In the end, Dunn got McCulley to commit to the Boilermakers. But after two seasons, in which the Boilermakers went to the NCAA Women's Final Four and the Elite Eight, McCulley transferred with her good friend Leslie Johnson to Western Kentucky.

Rascally Rabbit

The football team nearly upset third-ranked Michigan on October 31, 1992, opening a 17-7 halftime advantage before losing 24-17 at Ross-Ade Stadium.

But the highlight of the near miss was the exploits of a rabbit that got loose on the field during the third quarter. It raced up and down the field numerous times, crossing the goal line at the south end of the stadium on three occasions and triggering a mighty roar from the crowd of 38,021 before exiting through an open gate. Someone in the press box estimated that the hare rushed for 286 yards.

"We need to hire him as a running back," head coach Jim Colletto deadpanned afterwards.

The rascally rabbit was honored with an ESPY Award (Excellence in Sports Performance) as the "Outrageous Play of the Year."

Incoming

Purdue became the first team to beat Minnesota in Williams Arena during the 1993-94 season, and apparently one of the Golden Gophers' fans wasn't too pleased about it.

Immediately following the Boilermakers' 75-72 victory January 29, 1994, Glenn Robinson was hit in the head by a soft drink can that was thrown from the student section as Purdue was leaving the court.

He wasn't injured, but as the Boilermakers boarded their bus, Minnesota coach Clem Haskins came out of the arena and apologized to Robinson, Coach Gene Keady and the entire Purdue traveling party.

"He couldn't react the way he wanted to," teammate Cuonzo Martin said. "He's one of those guys that has a lot of fire inside and is ready to react at any time. That's the kind of guy you love playing with, because he was ready to do battle at all times."

No Need for a Locksmith

As the Boilermakers prepared to depart from Minneapolis on their charter airplane following a 75-72 upset over the Golden Gophers in 1994, they were waiting for their team meal to be delivered.

On this occasion, the team was going to enjoy pizzas during the trip home. When the pizza delivery man pulled up to the aircraft, he got out of his car and briefly greeted assistant coach Bruce Weber, who handled all the team's meals on the road.

Much to the embarrassment of the delivery man, he locked his keys in his car with it running and the pizzas inside.

After a hard-fought win, the players were craving some food, so once word spread throughout the aircraft about the crisis,

Glenn Robinson and Tim Ervin hopped out of their seats to see if they could help.

They asked the flight attendants for wire hangers and quickly made their way to the car. Within a matter of seconds, the two had gotten into the car and unlocked it. Needless to say, their teammates were much appreciative as they cheered when the two reboarded the plane.

Robinson was quick to turn to the few members of the media who always traveled with the team and say, "You didn't see that."

Minneapolis, We've Got a Problem

O ver the years the Boilermakers have had their share of travel difficulties, but one return trip home was a little more frightening than most any other.

On January 29, 1994, Purdue had a close encounter in the not-so-friendly skies on the return trip to West Lafayette. The Boilermakers' charter flight departed from the Minneapolis Airport, but had to return shortly after takeoff because of a mechanical problem.

The pilot radioed the control tower to prepare for an emergency landing, which is a common practice when aircraft encounter problems of any sort. Fire trucks stood by on the runway as the plane landed safely.

The problem concerned the landing gear in the plane's nose. After approximately an hour delay, the team departed again for the Purdue Airport, arriving two hours later than anticipated.

Fifth Time's a Charm

T he women's basketball team was 0-4 against No. 1-ranked teams when Penn State came to Mackey Arena on February 11, 1994, as the last remaining undefeated team in the nation.

Purdue used a 17-3 run over the last six minutes of the first half to lead 36-23 at halftime before the Lady Lions scored the first 12 points of the second half to make it a one-point game. Penn State later trailed by only one with less than a minute to go when Purdue put the ball into the hands of junior guard Cindy Lamping, who hit a running jumper with 31.7 seconds left and sealed a 57-54 victory.

Freshman Jannon Roland led the Boilermakers with 12 points off the bench, while Lamping scored 11 to go with four assists.

G-Rob's Sore Back Proved Costly

Perennial power Duke ended Purdue's quest for a national championship March 26, 1994, with a 69-60 win in the NCAA Tournament Southeast Regional final. But few realized at the time that Glenn Robinson was far from 100 percent healthy.

The game featured two of the country's premier players in Robinson and Grant Hill. All of the newspaper accounts following the game credited Hill and his teammates for shutting down the "Big Dog," but it was also Robinson's sore back that slowed him.

Robinson, the nation's leading scorer, played all but 20 seconds, matching his jersey number with a season-low 13 points (five in the second half), hitting just six of 22 shots and a game-high 13 rebounds. He missed all six three-pointers after hitting six of 10 from beyond the arc in a 44-point effort against Kansas two days earlier.

Robinson was rumored to have had the flu and back pains, but he dispelled those notions in the postgame press conference.

Robinson's teammate and close friend Cuonzo Martin, however, said No. 13 was in pain.

"He hurt his back against Kansas," Martin said. "Then we had a little horseplay going on that night [in the team hotel] before the Duke game. He really hurt his back then. There was some wrestling going on. We used to always wrestle as a team.

"That [sore back] took a lot out of him, but you can't make an excuse for him. He tried to play and didn't say anything about it. We lost the game and moved on."

How sore was Robinson's back? So sore that he had difficulty tying his shoes before the game and even received an injection to mask the pain prior to tipoff.

Getting a T.O. With Dicky V

At the peak of Dick Vitale mania, *Sports Illustrated*, in its March 7, 1994, edition, did an eight-page feature on him chronicling his popularity. A great majority of the piece showcased his January 18 visit to West Lafayette to call Purdue's overtime win over Indiana on ESPN.

There were a handful of photographs published taken during Vitale's trip to Mackey Arena, which accompanied the *SI* article. One of the shots showed *Gold & Black Illustrated* editor Doug Griffiths interviewing Vitale prior to the game while he was shaving in the men's restroom just to the east of the tunnel in Mackey. The photo caption read, "There's no time—or place—Vitale won't schmooze."

Celebrity Status

As Purdue was taking the court for its open practice for the 1994 NCAA Tournament Southeast Regional in Knoxville, Tennessee, Glenn Robinson caused quite a stir.

With his teammates already on the floor, Robinson made his way to the floor surrounded by television cameras. As he passed through the tunnel, hundreds of autograph seekers hung over the railing trying to get Robinson's attention. When he reached the court, the crowd cheered.

During the practice the crowd barked whenever the "Big Dog" touched the ball, occasionally drawing a smile from Robinson.

After the one-hour practice, Robinson obliged those in search of his autograph. There was such a scramble to get near Robinson that a youngster was hurt. Finally, after Robinson signed dozens of autographs, he made his way to the team bus. By the way, the injured boy did get his basketball autographed.

Throughout the 1993-94 season, Robinson was a marked man for autograph seekers. It was common for fans to brave the elements and wait for a chance to get his autograph when he was exiting or arriving at the team hotel or walking off the team bus for a game.

In January of 1994, as the Purdue players were getting off their charter plane at the airport in State College, Pennsylvania, a trio of youngsters braved the below-freezing conditions and 18 inches of snow in an attempt to get Robinson's autograph. They were armed with new basketballs and pens.

Shaking his head, Robinson obliged, inking the roundballs. The trio walked away, under the nose of the plane, comparing the All-American's signature.

An Atmosphere to Remember

The Hyatt Regency in Knoxville, Tennessee, was Purdue's team headquarters, and hundreds of Boilermaker fans turned it into West Lafayette South for the 1994 NCAA Tournament.

Pep rallies were held before each game as hundreds of followers filled the spacious hotel lobby. The Boilermaker faithful were treated to performances by the band and cheerleaders as well as special guest speakers. Television stations from Indiana took advantage of the environment for live reports.

Fans decked themselves and their cars out in anything gold and black. One fanatic even took his own version of "Big Dog" and had his animal dressed in the school colors. "Beware of the Dog" signs were everywhere, as were gold pompoms.

After Purdue's win over Kansas, the team returned to the hotel at approximately 1:30 a.m. The Boilermakers were led into a side door due to the overflow of fans awaiting their arrival. As the team entered the band played "Hail Purdue."

"I felt like a king walking through that hotel lobby," Cuonzo Martin said. "It was a great feeling. That was great fan support. I haven't seen anything like that since I've been playing or coaching. The fan support was at another level."

Tattooed

As an extra means of incentive, women's basketball coach Lin Dunn offered to get a tattoo if her 1993-94 team reached the NCAA Women's Final Four.

The Boilermakers did, and Dunn kept her word, although she had hoped her players would forget. Some seven months after Purdue made the Women's Final Four for the first time in school history, Dunn had the word "Final" and number "4" emblazoned above her right chest.

"I was kidding, and they were not," Dunn said. "It came back to haunt me the minute we beat Stanford [in the NCAA Tournament's West Regional final] because the chant was not 'Final Four,' 'Final Four,' but 'Tattoo,' 'Tattoo.'"

Known for doing whatever it takes to be successful, Dunn hardly learned her lesson. Eight years later, as head coach of the Seattle Storm of the WNBA, she agreed to dye her infamous gray, beehive hairdo blonde if her team made the playoffs.

Again, the players delivered, and All-Star center Lauren Jackson asked Dunn to switch from blonde to red, prompting many fans to show up at the Storm's first-ever home playoff game sporting red wigs. Dunn retired from coaching soon after the season and was spared the dye bottle. "But if I had stayed, of course I would have done it," she said.

"Baby Bark"

Leslie Johnson arrived at Purdue in 1993 as one of the nation's most heralded freshmen. She didn't disappoint, topping the team in scoring (18.5) and rebounding (9.1) en route to being named the National Freshman of the Year and an honorable mention All-American. Johnson was a key component in the Boilermakers sharing the Big Ten championship and advancing to the NCAA Women's Final Four for the first time in school history.

Johnson called herself "Baby Bark," after perennial NBA All-Star Charles Barkley. She even included the moniker when signing autographs. She had the same body composition as the robust Barkley, making the nickname more appropriate.

As a sophomore in 1994-95, Johnson battled injuries and illness before ultimately quitting the team. She played in just 14 games, averaging 10.9 points and 5.8 rebounds. Johnson transferred to Western Kentucky after the season.

Johnson's 628 points and 308 rebounds remain Purdue freshman season records. She also has the top two single-game scoring performances by a freshman—34 at Vanderbilt on December 5, 1993, and 32 against Northwestern on February 27, 1994.

Three for Four

D uring her career as a collegiate basketball player, Tonya Kirk shot only 28 percent from three-point range (57 of 207). But her triple against Stanford in the 1994 NCAA Tournament West Regional final stands as one of the biggest shots in school history.

The Boilermakers, despite being seeded No. 1, were underdogs to the home-standing and No. 2 seed Cardinal at Maples Pavilion. Stanford entered the game 10-0 at home in NCAA Tournament games and winners of 108 of their last 111 games in Maples overall.

After taking a 32-25 lead at halftime, Purdue watched Stanford get back into the game and tie it 36-all with 14 minutes remaining. That's when Kirk, then a sophomore, drained her three-pointer from the top of the key that gave the Boilermakers a lead they would never relinquish.

Stanford got within a single point three times, but Purdue opened a 64-55 advantage with less than three minutes to go and went on to an 82-65 victory and the school's first-ever trip to the Women's Final Four. It was the Cardinal's worst home-court loss in seven years.

Jennifer Jacoby led the Boilermakers with 20 points, including 10 of 12 from the free-throw line.

The Cardinal Rule of Recruiting

Y ou can credit assistant coach Bruce Weber for discovering Brian Cardinal in the tiny town of Tolono, Illinois, and convincing Coach Gene Keady to offer him a scholarship.

Illinois coach Lou Henson and his staff took a wait-and-see approach on Cardinal, despite the fact that his father, Rod, was the Fighting Illini's basketball athletic trainer. Henson wanted to see how Cardinal performed during his senior year at Unity High School before offering him a full scholarship. That strategy backfired on Henson, however, as Cardinal jumped at Purdue's offer.

He made Illinois pay from that day forward. Cardinal helped Purdue go 8-0 against the Illini from 1997 to 2000.

"I came from a small town and there were a lot of people who doubted me," recalled Cardinal, who scored 17 points and had 11 rebounds in his first Big Ten game at Illinois. "It was great to prove them wrong."

Weber still remembers seeing Cardinal for the first time. It was the spring of 1994, and Cardinal was preparing for his final year of high school hoops by playing in numerous AAU tournaments and making a name for himself amidst the staunch competition. By the end of the summer, however, the scrappy youngster was tapped out, having played in too many games.

"As the summer neared an end, his play worsened as the number of big-time coaches [who watched him] increased," Weber said. "He played three consecutive weeks without going home, and he was exhausted by the end. I remember seeing him in Columbus, Ohio, in the last event of the year, and I don't think he scored a bucket the entire weekend."

But Weber already had made up his mind. Cardinal had earned a scholarship to Purdue because of all the little things he did on the hardwood.

"He had a knack for getting the loose balls, grabbing a rebound he shouldn't have and diving on the floor," Weber said.

Once Cardinal arrived on the West Lafayette campus, he questioned whether or not he belonged at the big-time level.

"The funny thing about Brian was he never had very high self-esteem," Weber explained. "As a freshman, he just didn't think he was any good. He was good, and he just didn't know it."

It was prior to the start of his freshman season in 1995-96 that Cardinal, with the encouragement of the Boilermaker coaching staff, decided to redshirt.

During that season on the bench, Cardinal was so paranoid that Keady would insert him into a game, thus burning his redshirt season, that he didn't wear his uniform under his warmup. Instead, Cardinal wore just his underwear.

Thanks to Program Feature, Keyes Returned to Alma Mater

When Leroy Keyes was a Boilermaker, he was hungry to succeed. Nearly 30 years after his playing career at Purdue ended, he developed an appetite for coaching.

Keyes, voted the school's all-time greatest player in a fan poll taken in 1987, coached the game he loved while serving as president of the Penrose Park Youth Association in Philadelphia.

"I thought I was going to be the next coach at Purdue, and when they hired Jim Colletto, I was despondent and gave up coaching," Keyes said. "I said, 'If I can't come back to Purdue and coach, I don't want to coach anywhere in America.'"

Bob DeMoss, Purdue's head football coach from 1970 to 1972 who later went on to be an athletics department administrator, contacted Keyes in 1990 during the search for a new football coach. They wanted his recommendation for a new football coach. Keyes's response was, "[Give it to] me, I know football."

Keyes was listening to suggestions made by former players and alumni that he apply for the coaching position. His concern was that he felt no one in the athletics department took him seriously.

"I told Jim Colletto when I first met him, 'I wanted the same position that you have,'" Keyes admitted.

In March of 1995, Keyes got his wish in part. Colletto hired him as an assistant coach in charge of the running backs.

Colletto said he got the idea for hiring Keyes from reading a game program story that ran for the 1994 Purdue-Indiana game.

At the time he was hired, Keyes said, "I am ecstatic about coming back to Purdue. I'll be trying to live part of my dream."

Irish Continue Ducking Boilermakers

January 4, 1966, is a significant date in Boilermaker basketball history. That's the last time Purdue faced Notre Dame on the hardwood.

Despite the two schools playing every year in football, the two have not met in basketball since that winter night in South Bend.

Why haven't they played?

Through the years, Purdue has had the approach of "Why don't we play?"

Notre Dame's response seems to be, "Why should we?"

Notre Dame is closer to Purdue than any Big Ten schools. Just 105 miles separate the two campuses.

Former Purdue athletics director George King said, "At the time [1966], Johnny Dee was the coach at Notre Dame. There was one year left on our contract and it was to be a home game for us. But he called me and asked if I could relieve him of the next game, which was to be played at Purdue. He had too many games and said he would like to have a year's leave of absence and pick it up the following year. I agreed to that.

"The following year he called and said, 'We've got you all set to play up here.' I said, 'No, Johnny, you said you were coming here.' He refused and we never got together."

Notre Dame's former coach Digger Phelps, a good friend of former Indiana coach Bob Knight, used to say, "The roads don't lead from South Bend to West Lafayette." Yet the two schools' football teams never get lost making the annual trek.

Phelps was caught on the defensive by Dick Vitale, as an ESPN panel previewed the Purdue-Wisconsin-Green Bay first-round NCAA Tournament game in 1995.

Dickie V. predicted a Boilermaker victory and noted that Phelps might disagree. Vitale challenged the former Irish coach as to why he would never play Purdue.

"I just didn't want to lose twice in [the state of] Indiana [in the same season]," Phelps confessed as he quickly changed subjects. Phelps's Notre Dame teams annually played Knight's IU teams.

Coach Gene Keady often has been asked about the prospects of playing Notre Dame. The Boilermaker boss said he would play the Irish anywhere, any time. In fairness, if the series is to be renewed, he, along with Purdue, wants the first game to be played in Mackey Arena.

Upon Further Review

Following Purdue's 75-73 loss to Memphis in the second round of the 1995 NCAA Midwest Regional in Austin, Texas, the Boilermaker coaching staff sent Roy Hairston's jersey, a videotape and a quote from Tiger center Lorenzen Wright to Hank Nichols, the NCAA's head of officials.

The controversy centered around the Tigers' last-second game-winning shot. Forward David Vaughn grabbed an offensive rebound and scored on a putback with 1.6 seconds left to end Purdue's season. In the postgame press conference, Wright admitted to holding Hairston, enabling Vaughn to rebound guard Chris Garner's errant shot. Hairston noticed a hole had been torn in his jersey during a timeout with 1.1 ticks remaining.

"When Roy went up for the rebound, he [Vaughn] grabbed his shirt and he had a big hole in it," said Cuonzo Martin, who was a senior forward at the time, "and that was a thick jersey, but when you're talking about NCAA Tournament play, stuff like that happens. The ref doesn't want to make a call in that situation. It was a tough loss for us, and I will always remember it because it ended my college career."

"I saw the shot go up and then two Purdue players came in," Wright said. "I grabbed one player [Hairston] and I pinned the other one [Brandon Brantley] under my arm. Then I saw David get the ball and I held on until he got the shot off."

Two of the three officials, Tom Rucker and Eugene Monje, primarily worked Big Ten games during the regular season. Rucker had been officiating conference contests since 1972. Both were in position to make the call. The replay showed the blatant foul, as well as one official watching the ball in the air instead of the contact underneath, and television stations nationwide aired it.

The front page of *USA Today's* March 22 sports section pointed out Wright, saying, "The 6-foot-11 freshman prodigy helped beat Purdue with 10 points, eight rebounds, two steals and a timely tug on a jersey."

Had the officials seen the violation, Vaughn's basket would have been waved off, and Hairston or Brantley would have been shooting a pair of free throws with the score tied at 73 with less than two seconds left.

In April, Purdue heard back from the NCAA, which apologized for the officiating crew missing the call.

The Shot

Nobody gave the Purdue women's basketball team much of a chance when the Boilermakers played top-seeded and fifth-ranked Vanderbilt in the 1995 NCAA Tournament West Regional semifinals at Pauley Pavilion on the campus of UCLA in Los Angeles. After all, the Commodores had whipped the Boilermakers by 20 points during the regular season.

But Purdue built a 31-21 lead with nine minutes to go in the first half before settling for a 35-34 advantage at halftime. There were seven lead changes and four ties in the second half, with neither team leading by more than four points. Vanderbilt ultimately led 66-64 with eight seconds remaining and was at the free throw line with a chance to put the game away. But Lisa Ostrom missed the front end of the one-and-one. Tonya Kirk grabbed the rebound for the Boilermakers and got the ball in the hands of Jennifer Jacoby, who dribbled down the court and penetrated the lane before kicking the ball out to a wide-open Jannon Roland on the right wing. Roland, then a sophomore, calmly drained a three-pointer with one second left for a 67-66 victory.

Roland finished with 14 points, and "The Shot" was one of three nominees for an ESPY Award (Excellence in Sports Performance) in the category "College Basketball Play of the Year."

As a side note, the Purdue radio crew had technical difficulties with its equipment, and play-by-play announcer Tim Newton and color commentator Teri Moren were forced to call the game by passing a phone receiver back and forth.

Lovelace: In Your Face

As a junior in 1994-95, Stacey Lovelace of the women's basketball team was named the Big Ten Most Valuable Player, Big Ten Player of the Year and a Kodak All-American. She did it all for the Boilermakers, topping the team in scoring (14.2) rebounding (8.1), blocked shots (81) and steals (74).

Her shot blocking became legendary, as her total of 81 was more than seven Big Ten women's *teams* and four conference *men's teams*. Lovelace was Purdue's career leader with 174 blocks at the end of her junior season and remains the far-and-away leader with 220.

Lovelace also is the Boilermakers' career rebounds leader with 876 and one of only three players in school history to rank in the top 10 in career points, rebounds, blocks and steals. Joy Holmes (1988-91) and Katie Douglas (1998-2001) are the others.

O.J. Trial Takes Center Stage

It seemed everyone was tuned in to hear the historic verdict in the O.J. Simpson trial October 3, 1995, including members of the media who covered Boilermaker football.

At Purdue head coach Jim Colletto's press conference that

day, a majority of those who normally participated in the weekly teleconference were absent. One journalist present started his tape recorder and went to another room to watch the happenings on television. Once he returned he informed those attending the luncheon of the not-guilty verdict. Many were stunned, including Colletto, who shook his head when told.

Boilermaker running backs coach Leroy Keyes, who knew Simpson from their college playing days and beyond, said of the verdict, "It sends a message to society. You're not above being prosecuted for behaviors that go against the judicial system of this country. It showed O.J. Simpson is not outside of the law. I don't care how big we are, we're not that big. Twelve of his peers said he was not guilty, so based on that, I'm glad O.J. Simpson was found not guilty. I followed the case just like everyone all over the world.

"I'm sorry this had to come about. My heart goes out to members of the families who lost loved ones, but I hope O.J. can put his life back together and be the model citizen we've known him to be."

Keyes finished runner-up for the 1968 Heisman Trophy behind Simpson. The two first met during All-America team award ceremonies and were opponents in the 1968 East-West Shrine Bowl in Simpson's hometown of San Francisco. They kept in touch during their NFL days, but eventually parted ways.

Space "P"

The "P" link that hangs from the Old Oaken Bucket for the football team's 51-14 win over intrastate rival Indiana on November 24, 1995, has a unique "background," to say the least.

From October 18 to November 1, 1993, that "P" flew aboard the U.S. Space Shuttle Columbia, with her crew of seven astronauts. Columbia completed 225 orbits of the Earth while traveling nearly 5.9 million miles. It took off from Kennedy Space Center in Florida and landed at Edwards Air Force Base in California.

Mission STS-58 had two other, more distinguished Boilermaker ties—commander John E. Blaha earned a master's degree in astronautical engineering from Purdue in 1966, while mission specialist David Wolf received a bachelor's degree in electrical engineering from Purdue in 1978. It was the 89th U.S. human space flight conducted by NASA.

The space "P" had to wait to be linked to the bucket until 1995 because the Boilermakers lost both the 1993 and 1994 meetings with the Hoosiers.

On February 1, 2003, Columbia and her crew of seven astronauts on mission STS-107 (the 28th flight of the shuttle) perished during its re-entry into the Earth's atmosphere.

When Push Comes to Shove

Pound for pound, football star Mike Alstott was one of Purdue's greatest athletes ever. His work ethic during the offseason was unparalleled.

The six-foot-two, 240-pounder was obsessed with making himself better each day.

One of the ways he improved physically was with a unique training ritual. During the summer prior to his senior season, Alstott pushed a Jeep 100 yards, two nights a week, to strengthen his arms and legs. This blue-collar ritual was nothing new for Alstott.

The summer prior to his senior year at Joliet (Illinois) Catholic

High School, Alstott pushed a station wagon down the street in front of his house. A friend steered while Alstott pushed the vehicle 100 yards, eight times a day. He also ran 40-yard sprints 20 times a day while dragging two Ford Bronco tires with a 15-foot rope tied to a weight belt around his waist.

So was it any wonder that Alstott was the strongest player on the 1995 Boilermaker team? He bench-pressed 420 pounds, squatted 575, ran the 40-yard dash in 4.74, had a vertical jump of 36.5 inches and had just 10 percent body fat.

That's probably why Alstott gave coaches like Minnesota's Jim Wacker "nightmares." Wacker said, "Alstott has got our kids psyched out. He runs over them, through them and outruns them."

Michigan nose tackle Jason Horn said, "If you tackle him high, he will run you over. If you tackle him low, he'll put his knee in your facemask and knock your helmet off. He is one of those guys that can have guys hanging on his back and still keep running."

Later in the 1995 season, *Sports Illustrated* came to West Lafayette to do a story and photo shoot with Alstott. The magazine took photos of Alstott and roommate Jayme Washel pushing the fullback's Jeep.

Dewey-ing It Right

Carol Dewey became a coaching legend during her 20 seasons at the helm of the volleyball program. From 1975 to 1995, she routinely produced winning teams and successful student-athletes.

With a record of 469-249, only men's basketball coach Gene Keady has won more games in Purdue history. Sixteen of Dewey's teams posted winning seasons, and she piloted the Boilermakers to four Big Ten championships, six 30-win seasons and nine postseason national tournament berths. Most of her teams at the same time compiled an overall grade-point average over 3.0 on

Mike Alstott

a 4.0 scale.

In November of 1991, Dewey was named recipient of the M. Beverley Stone Award by Purdue's chapter of Omicron Delta Kappa, a national leadership honorary. The award is presented annually to the Purdue staff person in a noncounseling position who provides counseling, support and mentoring to Purdue students, and the recipient makes a commitment to students, provides leadership and demonstrates a love for the university and campus community. Nothing more accurately describes Dewey, who was inducted into the Purdue Intercollegiate Athletics Hall of Fame in 2003.

One of her players, Jan (Hoosline) Mickey, who also served as a graduate assistant under Dewey, perhaps said it best: "What I learned in the classroom was important, but what I learned from the volleyball program was instrumental."

Beer or Wine

From 1991 to 1995, Tom Schott worked with the women's volleyball and basketball teams as assistant sports information director. He often was asked to compare the two head coaches, prim and proper Carol Dewey and wild and crazy Lin Dunn. "Let me explain it this way," Schott liked to say. "When Carol invited you over to her house, she served cheese and crackers and a nice glass of wine. When Lin had you over, it was microwave popcorn and light beer in a can."

Perfect Against IU

During her nine seasons at Purdue, Lin Dunn built the women's basketball program into a national power. The Boilermakers averaged 23 wins per season, won three Big Ten championships and played in seven NCAA Tournaments, reaching the Women's Final Four in 1994.

Perhaps Dunn's most impressive accomplishment, however, was going a perfect 18-0 against intrastate rival Indiana. While never losing to the Hoosiers, the Boilermakers did endure a few close encounters. None were closer than what proved to be Dunn's final game against Indiana.

It was February 9, 1996, and the Boilermakers were in the midst of a roller-coaster campaign. The game was a microcosm of the season, as Purdue led 63-49 with six minutes to go before Indiana went on a 17-2 run to take a 66-65 advantage with

Carol Dewey

6.6 seconds left. After both teams called time outs, Tonya Kirk inbounded the ball to junior Jannon Roland, who drove the length of the court and nailed a six-foot running jumper at the buzzer to give the Boilermakers a miraculous 67-66 victory.

The win was Dunn's 200th at Purdue. She had a record of 28-1 against all schools from the state of Indiana, losing only to Notre Dame in the first round of the 1996 NCAA Tournament in her last game at the helm of the Boilermakers. One week after the 73-60 loss, Dunn's contract was not renewed.

Different School, Different Result

I n the championship game of the 1988 National Women's Invitational Tournament, DePaul handily beat Purdue 83-55. The Blue Demons were coached by Jim Izard, who after the season was hired at Indiana. Story has it that Izard boasted about beating the Boilermakers as part of his candidacy. Over the next eight seasons, Izard was 0-16 against Purdue. He then won three in a row before losing the next five, making Izard's record against the Boilermakers with Indiana a paltry 3-21.

No Hospitality

P urdue didn't exactly feel at home in Indiana's Assembly Hall prior to the game played in 1996.

As the Boilermakers came out to warm up, they discovered the balls weren't completely inflated and had an unusual slickness to them. Forward Herb Dove said it was hard to dribble and make cuts with the flat balls.

In addition, following their 74-72 dramatic win over the Hoosiers, the Boilermaker players weren't provided with enough towels after showering.

"Those things were motivating factors for us," senior forward Justin Jennings said. "We just had to come out and play and forget about all those other things. Coach [Gene Keady] always says expect the unexpected. Anything can happen down here."

One strange happening occurred early in the game. Indiana had three dunks in the first 3:35, and each time, the rim collapsed it had to be pushed back up. Finally, after the Purdue coaching staff complained, during a timeout at the 15:50 mark, the officials ordered the rim to be replaced.

Boilermaker fans and players wondered if the rim was loosened to keep Purdue from pushing the ball up the floor after an

IU basket. That would also help prevent the Hoosiers from getting too winded. After all, in the game IU used only eight players, three of whom didn't see more than eight minutes of action.

Rumor also had it that Bob Knight guaranteed a win over Purdue, saying if the Boilermakers won, he would give them two of the Hoosiers' national championship banners.

No "I" in Team

After quarterback John Reeves spent 11 days in Lafayette's Home Hospital from February 10 to 21, 1996, with bacterial meningitis, a potentially lethal disease, his football career was in serious peril, to say the least.

But the Bradenton, Florida, native defied the odds.

Reeves lost 21 pounds and was on death's door during the illness. Amazingly, he battled back to start in five midseason games during the 1996 season.

When Joe Tiller took over the Purdue program following the 1996 season, Reeves had to practically start over despite playing part time at quarterback in Coach Jim Colletto's last year with the Boilermakers. Reeves impressed Tiller during spring practice enough to be named starting quarterback as the team entered its two-a-days in August of 1997.

However, Reeves lost his starting job to Billy Dicken prior to the opener against Toledo.

Rather than sulk, Reeves did something not many people of his age would do. He paid Tiller a visit in his office to ask him if he could change positions in order to get on the field.

"It became apparent after a week of two-a-days that Billy had moved ahead of John," Tiller recalled. "John came into me and said, 'Coach, I know Billy is the better quarterback than I am right now. I don't have any hard feelings. If you want to move me somewhere else and there's some way for me to get on the field and help the team, I'm willing to do that.'

"John's willingness to make that move probably had as much to do with us having the successful year we had as anything. That helped our team immeasurably."

Reeves was moved to defensive back and ultimately helped the Boilermakers on special teams in 1997.

One year later, Reeves did something even more remarkable in the eyes of Tiller. He earned an additional year of eligibility by graduating from Purdue in four years. Why was that out of the ordinary? Because Reeves arrived at Purdue as a Proposition 48 casualty and had to sit out his freshman season.

After passing 42 hours in a calendar year, he graduated in August of 1998 and was moved to linebacker during the 1998 season.

Reeves went on to play two seasons with the San Diego Chargers, adding another chapter to one of the greatest stories of determination ever told in Purdue history.

Thought for the Day

At every practice during her nine-year stint at Purdue, women's basketball coach Lin Dunn greeted her players with a "Thought for the Day."

Here's a sampling:

"It's amazing what we can accomplish when no one cares who gets the credit."

"Pick your friends, but not to pieces."

"The more you help others, the more you help yourself."

"When you're green with envy, you're ripe for trouble."

"Even a mosquito doesn't get a pat on the back until it starts working."

Dunn's personal favorite: "The three most important bones—the wishbone: you've got to have a dream; the funny bone: laughter is a tranquilizer with no side effects; and the backbone: if you don't stand for something, you will fall for anything!"

Oh, Canada!

Of all the basketball prospects that Purdue has recruited and that have gone elsewhere over the years, one of the ones that hurt the most was losing six-foot-10, 233-pound Jamaal Magloire, a Toronto, Canada, native, to Kentucky. He was considered the second best prospect at center in the high school ranks behind All-American Jermaine O'Neal, who entered the NBA out of high school.

In early May of 1996, the Boilermaker coaching staff thought they had landed one of North America's best post prospects, only to find out less than 10 days later he was going to Kentucky.

Sources close to the Boilermaker program said Magloire's parents, who visited Purdue May 10 to 12, told the Purdue coaching staff that their son would attend Purdue in the fall. Magloire even contacted two Purdue coaches at their homes May 14, telling them he was going to sign with the Boilermakers during the spring signing period. He called Coach Gene Keady the following night, three hours after speaking to Kentucky coach Rick Pitino, and said the same thing.

Less than a week before his announcement, which was made at a press conference May 21, he told the *Norwich (Connecticut) Bulletin,* "Kentucky has been putting pressure on me, but I need to do what's right for me."

As late as May 17, sources close to the Kentucky program weren't optimistic about Magloire signing with the Wildcats and called Purdue the odds-on favorite. Even recruiting analyst Bob Gibbons thought Purdue was a lock to get Magloire's services. Gibbons's 900-line said Magloire would sign with Purdue. On May 16, the *Toronto Sun* reported that Magloire was leaning heavily toward Purdue. A day later, the sports director at Lexington's CBS affiliate said Magloire was headed to Purdue.

The Boilermaker coaching staff became pessimistic May 17 when they failed to receive Magloire's national letter of intent on the designated day.

Interestingly enough, Magloire's parents didn't visit Kentucky.

Magloire, who now plays for the NBA's New Orleans Hornets, said he decided on UK because he could play right away. Purdue told him he would likely start, too. After all, the Boilermaker coaches wanted to move Brad Miller to power forward and use Luther Clay to back up Miller and Magloire.

Why did Kentucky get Magloire? One thing is for certain, hiring Magloire's high school coach, Simeon Mars, for an administrative assistant position allowing him to sit on the bench certainly didn't hurt the Wildcats.

Corissa: Simply the Best

Simply stated, Corissa Yasen is the best female athlete in Purdue history. In track and field, competing in the high jump, heptathlon and pentathlon, Yasen was a nine-time All-American, 10-time Big Ten champion and four-time team Most Valuable Player. Her crown jewel was winning the 1996 national championship in the heptathlon, becoming Purdue's first female NCAA champion.

Following her four years on the oval, she used her fifth year of eligibility to compete with the Purdue women's basketball team while completing her pharmacy degree. The Boilermakers, under first-year coach Nell Fortner, had been depleted by transfers following the departure of Lin Dunn and had just three returning letter winners.

Yasen had not played the sport since high school, but nevertheless became a starter and went on to earn honorable mention All-Big Ten recognition after averaging 11.4 points and 6.2 rebounds to go with 18 blocked shots and 66 steals. She was one of only two players in the conference to rank in the top 10 in both blocks and steals. Yasen clearly was instrumental in the Boilermakers sharing the conference championship and earning a bid to the NCAA Tournament.

Yasen, who was named Purdue's Female Athlete of the Year in

1995 and 1996, was a unanimous selection to the Intercollegiate Athletics Hall of Fame in 2003, her first year of eligibility.

Tragically, Yasen, who graduated with a degree in pharmacy, was found dead in her Coeur d'Alene, Idaho, home May 13, 2001. She was only 27.

"Citizen Pain"

During the 1996-97 season, redshirt freshman forward Brian Cardinal had several nicknames given to him.

He was called "Alien" and "Redbird," and then was dubbed "Citizen Pain."

The Lafayette *Journal and Courier* asked its readers for suggestions for a nickname for Cardinal, who was known for his scrappy, hustling style of play.

There were more than 260 responses. The nickname selected, "Citizen Pain," was submitted by Zac Laugheed, who was a seventh grader at Klondike Middle School in Lafayette.

Over the course of his playing career, Cardinal developed quite a reputation for the way he played the game.

In his freshman year in a game at Indiana, he dove for a loose ball and collided with press row, positioned along one of the sidelines. Cardinal crashed into *Indianapolis Star/News* reporter Curt Cavin's laptop and broke it.

Broxsie a Bizarre One

One of the more bizarre recruiting stories involving Purdue occurred in the spring of 1997. That year the Boilermakers exerted a tremendous amount of effort trying to get six-foot-10, 220-pound forward Antoine Broxsie from Tampa, Florida.

Broxsie narrowed his list to Purdue, Nebraska and Minnesota.

He eventually signed to play for Clem Haskins's Golden Gophers. Broxsie said he dreamt about playing at Purdue and in Mackey Arena. However, his mother wanted him to be a Cornhusker even though she didn't come with him when he visited the West Lafayette campus March 7 to 9. Broxsie said as a compromise the two agreed on Minnesota. According to Broxsie, who admitted being very religious, he turned to God to help him with his decision.

On May 16, one day after the last day high school players could sign their national letters of intent and still have them be legally binding, Minnesota's sports information department sent out a press release announcing Broxsie had signed with the Gophers.

However, later that afternoon when Broxsie was contacted, he didn't sound happy with his decision.

"I made a decision [to sign with Minnesota] last night, and I think it was the wrong decision," Broxsie said. "I'm not happy with it."

When he was asked if he sent Minnesota his letter of intent, Broxsie said, "I don't know yet. I need to ask my mom."

Then Broxsie was told the Gopher basketball office had his letter. "They couldn't have it yet because I haven't even put it in the mail yet.

"I really wanted to come to Purdue. I just felt like that was the place for me to be. That's really where I want to go."

As things turned out, Broxsie didn't play much at Minnesota in a program steeped in controversy thanks to academic fraud.

Hair-Raising Humor

If Joe Tiller wasn't a successful college football coach, he undoubtedly could make a living as a stand-up comedian. A darn good living. No matter what the audience, he gets the listeners rolling with his quick wit. One of his favorite openers is to talk about his lack of hair. "God created all these heads," he says. "The ones he was embarrassed by, he covered with hair.

"But truthfully I like my wife's explanation better," he continues. "She refers to me as a solar-powered sex machine."

A Recruiting Brees

Joe Tiller and his coaching staff never could have imagined what kind of player they signed in February of 1997, when they inked quarterback Drew Brees from Westlake High School in Austin, Texas.

Growing up in the Lone Star State, Brees admitted he wanted to play for one of the in-state schools. His parents attended Texas A&M, and he would have liked to follow in their footsteps.

"I wanted to go to A&M," said Brees, who led Westlake High School to a 16-0 record and the Class 5A (big school) 1996 Texas state championship en route to being named the state's Most Valuable Offensive Player. "But I knew they really didn't like me."

Despite throwing for 3,528 yards (completing 63.4 percent of his passes) and 31 touchdowns as a prep senior, the Aggies, as well as the University of Texas, were turned off by Brees's six-foot-one size and the fact that he had suffered a torn anterior cruciate ligament in his knee during the playoffs at the end of his junior season.

Brees narrowed his choices down to Kentucky and Purdue, the only two high-profile schools he officially visited (as well as Brown). He said his final decision came down to academics.

"Purdue is known for its academic reputation," said Brees after signing with the Boilermakers. "I want to take that Purdue degree back home and work there after I graduate."

"Can we win with Drew Brees? I certainly hope so," offensive coordinator Jim Chaney said.

Brees won all right. As the Boilermakers' three-year starter, he was 24-13 overall, 16-8 in the Big Ten, and took Purdue to three bowls. In addition, he left Purdue as the Big Ten's most prolific passer.

Feeling Knight's Wrath

After redshirt freshman forward Brian Cardinal scored a career-high 25 points against Indiana in an 89-87 overtime win against the Hoosiers on February 18, 1997, in Assembly Hall, IU coach Bob Knight went out of his way to shake Cardinal's hand.

When *Gold & Black Illustrated* editor Doug Griffiths asked Knight in the postgame press conference to comment on Cardinal's play, the Hoosier boss said, "Cardinal played very good. He's a very good player. Are you not capable of writing about it yourself?"

Griffiths responded, "Very capable."

Knight fired back, "Well then, write it."

Griffiths said, "I will."

A Defining Moment

Joe Tiller had nine wins in his first season at Purdue and has had many more since then in West Lafayette. But the one victory that he continues to say was the turning point for the program was his first, September 13, 1997, against No. 12 Notre Dame in Ross-Ade Stadium.

Not only had the Boilermakers not beaten the Fighting Irish since 1985, but they were coming off a season-opening loss at Toledo 36-22 a week earlier.

Few, if anybody, gave Tiller's team much of a chance against Notre Dame.

One of those doubters was former Purdue head coach Jim Colletto, who made his first visit to Ross-Ade Stadium since

Drew Brees

leaving the Boilermaker program and joining the Notre Dame staff as offensive coordinator and offensive line coach.

It turned out to be an unhappy return for Colletto to his old stomping ground. Tiller's Boilermakers shocked Colletto, the heavily favored Irish and an ABC television audience.

Purdue never trailed in the game. A Notre Dame touchdown with just under two minutes left trimmed Purdue's lead to 21-17, but the Boilermakers recovered the ensuing onside kick. Running back Kendall Matthews finished the scoring on a two-yard scamper to make it 28-17.

Quarterback Billy Dicken was sensational. He completed 26 of 38 passes for 352 passes, as the Boilermakers racked up 485 yards and 25 first downs.

Purdue students stormed the field to celebrate their team's improbable victory.

Amazing Comeback(s)

On November 8, 1997, the football team trailed Michigan State 21-10 with 2:13 left at Ross-Ade Stadium. The Boilermakers appeared headed for a second straight loss after winning six of their first seven games under new coach Joe Tiller.

But Leo Perez blocked a 39-yard field goal attempt by the Spartans, and Rosevelt Colvin returned it 62 yards for a touchdown, pulling Purdue within 21-16. After a failed two-point conversion, the Boilermakers recovered an onside kick on their own 45-yard line with two minutes to go. Senior quarterback Billy Dicken then marched Purdue down the field, and Edwin Watson scored the game-winning touchdown on a three-yard plunge with 40 seconds left. The Spartans still had a chance, but their 43-yard field goal missed with three seconds on the clock, giving Purdue an improbable 22-21 victory.

"Our chances of winning were slim to none," Tiller recalls. "The thing I remember most was how many people left the stadium, then after the fact, hearing how many people came back to the stadium. If I could, I probably would have left with them. To block a kick, return it for a touchdown, recover an onside kick and score, it's almost unfathomable. That was an unbelievable game."

One year later—on November 14, 1998—Purdue trailed Michigan State 24-13 with less than seven minutes to go and pulled out a 25-24 victory. This time, a blocked punt by Todd Stelma set up the fantastic finish, and Drew Brees hooked up with Isaac Jones on a game-winning six-yard touchdown pass with 1:21 remaining. It clearly was déjà vu all over again.

Coaching Greatness

Joe Tiller could have run for mayor of West Lafayette following the 1997 football season. In his first season as head coach at Purdue, he piloted the Boilermakers to a 9-3 record, including a victory over Oklahoma State in the Alamo Bowl. Pretty amazing considering the program had just one winning season (with the help of a forfeit victory) and no bowl game appearances since 1984. Along the way, the Boilermakers snapped an 11-game losing streak to intrastate rival and perennial national power Notre Dame.

Naturally, his success put Tiller up for numerous postseason coaching awards. He was named national Coach of the Year by both *Football News* and *Kickoff* magazines and was one of six finalists for the same honor by the American Football Coaches Association. He didn't win that one, and following the banquet honoring the finalists, Tiller rhetorically asked his wife, Arnette, "Do you know how many great coaches there are in college football?"

"One less than you do," she said.

You're a Grand Ol' Flag

As you walk into Coach Joe Tiller's office on the third floor of the Mollenkopf Athletic Facility, you will quickly notice a large black flag hanging on one of the walls. The flag has gold letters on it, which spell "P-U-R-D-U-E."

There's a plaque in Tiller's office just to the right of the flag

Joe Tiller

that describes the importance of the flag.

It reads, "This pennant (liberated from Ross-Ade Stadium in 1948) was gifted to Joe Tiller from its keeper, L. Michael Ream."

The pennant was "liberated" from the stadium following a 39-0 win over Indiana. It was taken from one of Ross-Ade's flag poles.

For a period of time, the pennant, which was sent to Tiller following the 1998 season, was placed in a safe deposit box so that moisture and humidity wouldn't ruin it.

"I didn't really know how to respond to it when it first arrived," Tiller said.

"I felt like I should send it back. Obviously, it was sent to me because the person that had it felt like it needed to be at Purdue and not in their possession."

Boiler Up!

In an attempt to bring more enthusiasm to football games at Ross-Ade Stadium, Head Coach Joe Tiller's wife, Arnette, came up with the phrase "Boiler Up." It immediately caught on and has remained a constant, even unofficially being incorporated into the Purdue fight song, "Hail Purdue."

What Arnette didn't know at the time of Boiler Up's origin was that in the days of steam-powered locomotives, when the fireman got the fire in the coal box hot enough for the engine to run, he would exclaim "Boiler's up!"

Drew Who?

Quarterback Drew Brees was a member of the first recruiting class signed by head coach Joe Tiller and his staff in February of 1997. Although a knee injury sustained during his junior year of high school resulted in all the major Texas schools backing off on the Austin native, the Boilermakers figured they just might have lucked into a pretty good prospect.

Brees saw limited action during the 1997 season as Billy Dicken's backup, and Tiller and Co. were not absolutely convinced he was the heir apparent. So they went out and signed a junior college player, David Edgerton, out of Garden City (Kansas) Community College.

Of course, Brees ended up working out, rewriting the Purdue and Big Ten records books. Edgerton, meanwhile, appeared sparingly in 12 games during his three years at Purdue, attempting 29 passes.

Topping Tennessee

The women's basketball team spent nearly every waking moment leading up to the 1998-99 season opener against perennial power Tennessee trying to figure out a way to beat Tennessee. The commitment paid off.

The Lady Vols invaded Mackey Arena on November 15, 1998, as the defending national champion and sporting a 46-game winning streak. But fifth-ranked Purdue conquered No. 1 Tennessee, posting a 78-68 victory in front of 11,788 fans and an ESPN national television audience in the State Farm Tipoff Classic.

"Purdue played very well today and played smart," legendary Tennessee head coach Pat Summit said afterward. "They picked our defense apart. They were more aggressive than we were. Our defense had very little influence on the Purdue offense."

Senior Stephanie White led the Boilermakers with 24 points, while sophomore Camille Cooper had a then-career high of 18 points. Freshman Kelly Komara, playing her first collegiate game, sparked Purdue with eight points off the bench, subbing for the foul-plagued Ukari Figgs.

The Boilermakers, who led 46-33 at halftime, dominated the Lady Vols in two significant categories, outrebounding them 36-25 and holding a 26-3 advantage in points off the bench.

The day after the victory, Purdue moved to No. 1 in the *Associated Press* national poll for the first time in school history. The Boilermakers' previous highest position was No. 2 in the 1994-95 preseason poll. It marked the first time any Purdue team was ranked at the top since 1968, when the football team enjoyed five weeks at No. 1.

Purdue's Version of "The Drive"

Purdue's stunning 37-34 win on December 29, 1998, over No. 4 Kansas State in the Alamo Bowl is one Boilermaker fans will cherish forever.

Few people gave Purdue much of a chance to upset K-State. After all, just a few weeks earlier the Wildcats were in the national championship hunt with an 11-0 record until a 36-33 double-overtime loss to Texas A&M in the Big 12 Championship Game on December 5.

The Boilermakers, a 13-point underdog, didn't listen to the critics or the oddsmakers. In going out and taking care of business, the Old Gold and Black posted its first win over a top five team away from West Lafayette since 1974.

Trailing by four points with less than 90 seconds remaining in the game, the unranked Boilermakers drove 80 yards in 54 seconds for a touchdown in the final minute to shock the Wildcats in the Alamodome. The drive was one of the most memorable in Purdue football history. The last-minute drive put quarterback Drew Brees on everybody's 1999 Heisman Trophy candidates list.

Brees threw a 24-yard touchdown pass to Isaac Jones with just 30 seconds remaining, sending the nearly 15,000 Boilermaker fans in attendance into a frenzy.

On the game-winning touchdown seen by 60,780 fans, of which about 30,000 were cheering for K-State, Jones beat Wildcat defensive back Dyshod Carter and made an exceptional over-the-shoulder catch while falling down.

The play was one Purdue had run frequently.

"It was a fade route to No. 2 [second receiver]," offensive coordinator Jim Chaney explained. "It gave Drew the ability to go to the fade or the post on the backside. Isaac ran it well, and Brees had the confidence in him."

"It was an absolutely perfect throw, a great catch and great concentration on the catch," Tiller said. "I don't know if the throw was more impressive than the catch or the catch was more

Stephanie White

impressive than the throw."

A couple of things made the catch even more impressive. Jones had been hobbled throughout the game with an ankle injury yet he was able to get behind Carter. In addition, Jones admitted losing the ball in the Alamodome lights.

"He made a play when we had to have one," Tiller said.

"I've probably not been around a bigger win. If you coach

long enough and you get lucky enough, you're around some pretty good wins over the years. We've been around some pretty good wins, but certainly this is one to remember."

Purdue nearly let the game slip away. It led 30-20 with 6:44 to play, only to see the Wildcats take the lead with less than two minutes to play.

The game-winning drive started with two incompletions. On third and 10, Brees hit receiver Chris Daniels over the middle. He stretched for the first down, giving Purdue the ball on its 31. On the next play, Brees's pass was high to receiver Randall Lane, but the Chicago native went up and got it for a 19-yard pickup to midfield. Then K-State was penalized 15 yards for pass interference and Purdue was at the Wildcat 35. Following the penalty, Brees scrambled up the middle and cut right before being knocked out of bounds for an 11-yard pickup. That run set up the TD pass on the very next play.

"They were playing a softer zone coverage at the end than they played the entire game," said Brees, who completed 25 of 53 passes for 230 yards. "We were able to complete more things underneath and downfield."

"The coaches called the right plays and we were able to execute," Jones said.

K-State defensive coordinator Mike Stoops said his players were fatigued on the game-winning drive. "We had a few breakdowns and we were tired. Our execution broke down on that last drive."

Purdue's defense put forth an effort that was one of the finest in school history. The Boilermakers scored 20 points off of four K-State turnovers, including three fumbles.

Purdue's defense allowed just one first down in the first quarter, and K-State had just two scoring drives longer than 28 yards. An incredible effort considering the Wildcats entered the game leading the nation in scoring, averaging 48 points per game, and ranked ninth nationally in total offense (averaging 478.5 yards). K-State had just 13 points after three quarters (seven came due to a recovered fumbled punt snap in the end zone). The Wildcats were held to just 308 total yards.

"We had done so many good things in that game against a really superior football team," Tiller said. "I had actually started to gather my thoughts on how I was going to talk to the media [if we had lost]."

Win One for Ukari

Spirits were high in the women's basketball offices on Monday and Tuesday, February 8 and 9, 1999. The Boilermakers were preparing to travel to Penn State to take on the rival Lady Lions on Friday night and, with a win, clinch the Big Ten championship.

But on Wednesday, the grandmother of senior point guard and team leader Ukari Figgs died suddenly, casting a pall over the program. Figgs immediately left to be with her family in Lexington, Kentucky, but vowed to rejoin her teammates in State College, Pennsylvania.

She made it, but it wasn't easy. Flying from Lexington to Pittsburgh was no problem, but Figgs's flight from Pittsburgh to State College was cancelled. So she took a three-hour cab ride and arrived at the team hotel just hours before tipoff.

The Boilermakers, ranked No. 2 nationally, appeared inspired by Figgs's devotion, but still had to overcome the 15th-ranked Lady Lions. Katie Douglas sent the game into overtime with a jump shot with 3.3 seconds left. Figgs then went up to her and asked, "Katie, will you win this game for me?"

Sure enough, Douglas scored a layup with 8.6 seconds left in overtime to give the Boilermakers a 76-74 victory and the fifth Big Ten title in the program's history.

"The team understood what I've been through this week," said Figgs, who scored 21 points. "I knew it was important for me to be here for my team. I have to give credit to God, who gave me the strength to play."

Figgs's grandmother, Ida, surely was smiling.

Project Perfect

At 16-0, the 1998-99 Boilermakers became just the second Big Ten women's basketball team to go undefeated in conference play. Ohio State went 18-0 during the 1984-85 season. Only 12 Big Ten men's teams have accomplished the feat in 97 seasons of conference play; most recently, Indiana at 18-0 in both 1974-75 and 1975-76.

Pur-duke

There may never be a more compelling story in women's basketball history than the 1999 national championship game between Purdue and Duke. The Boilermakers were led by senior guards Ukari Figgs and Stephanie White, while the Blue Devils featured guard Nicole Erickson and center Michele VanGorp. All four had been teammates at Purdue in 1995-96.

Erickson and VanGorp transferred following their freshman year when head coach Lin Dunn's contract was not renewed. Coaching Duke was Gail Goestenkors, who had been Dunn's assistant from 1988 to 1992. The Boilermakers won 62-45, with Figgs, White, Erickson and VanGorp all being named to the All-Final Four team.

Ms. Durability

Stephanie White holds the Purdue women's basketball record for most career minutes played with 4,398. She never missed a game in her four seasons (1995-96 to 1998-99), starting all 137 of the Boilermakers' contests and averaging 32 minutes per game.

White, in fact, never missed any time on the court because of injury, until, as fate would have it, her final game—against Duke in the 1999 national championship game. With four minutes left, White went down with a severely sprained left ankle and did not return. The Boilermakers led 47-42 when she left and proceeded to go on a 13-0 run en route to beating the Blue Devils 62-45.

White also holds the top two spots for school season minutes with 1,258 in 1998-99 and 1,246 in 1997-98.

Steph's Stats

Fans in Warren County, Indiana, didn't have to read the newspaper, listen to the radio or watch television to learn about the exploits of their favorite daughter, basketball star Stephanie White. Following every game, the marquee at the Powell Home Center on U.S. Highway 28 would "advertise" Steph's stats in bright red neon lights.

Coaching Merry-Go-Round

On March 23, 1996, athletics director Morgan Burke announced that the contract of women's basketball coach Lin Dunn was not being renewed. He cited his desire for the program to go "in a different direction."

Burke, however, never could have imagined the bizarre direction the Boilermakers were headed. Although the program never skipped a beat in terms of on-court success, it took three years to finally stabilize it.

First, Nell Fortner was hired, and she led Purdue to a Big Ten co-championship in 1996-97 but then left to head the U.S. Olympic Team. She was replaced by her top assistant coach,

Katie Douglas

Carolyn Peck, who piloted the Boilermakers to the Big Ten Tournament title in 1997-98 and the NCAA championship in 1998-99. But then Peck departed to become head coach and general manager of the Orlando Miracle of the WNBA.

So, on April 2, 1999, Kristy Curry was introduced to become the Boilermakers' third coach in four seasons and fourth in five.

She has stabilized the program over the last four years while winning two Big Ten regular-season crowns and two conference tournament titles and reaching the NCAA championship game in 2001.

There were two common denominators with Fortner, Peck and Curry: assistant coaches Kerry Cremeans and Pam Stackhouse, whose character, enthusiasm and love for Purdue kept the program heading in the *right* direction.

Hail to the Chief

President Bill Clinton honored the 1999 national championship women's basketball team at the White House on the afternoon of October 14, 1999. Head coach Carolyn Peck and team captains Ukari Figgs and Stephanie White presented the president with a Purdue home white jersey decked out with the name Clinton and the No. 1.

During the ceremony in the East Room—for which the Boilermakers stood on risers behind the president—Clinton recounted a conversation with Al Gore after Purdue's season-opening victory over Tennessee. Gore had suggested that the Lady Vols lost because of an off night, but Clinton said: "I don't think so, Al. That Purdue team is great. And I was right."

Afterward, Clinton posed for photos, gave away his notecards as souvenirs and visited with Billy Ray and Gloria Young, the parents of former player Tiffany Young. Tiffany had been tragically killed by a drunken driver in an automobile accident on July 31, 1999.

Before leaving the White House, the Boilermakers got to spend a few minutes with the Clinton's cat, Socks, and dog, Buddy.

The day also included a stop at the Senate for a visit with Indiana senators Evan Bayh and Richard Lugar.

Ukari Figgs

The Long Road Back

Mike Turner was one of the nation's top triple jumpers,
but that changed April 1, 1999.

Carolyn Peck

Running through training exercises as he had done thousands of times before in his successful career, Turner came down awkwardly on his leg during a pop-up drill.

"I heard about six pops," Turner said, "and I knew something was very, very wrong."

Purdue assistant track and field coach Lissa Olson wasn't aware of the seriousness of the injury at first.

"He was lying in the pit, and when I got over there I

realized it was serious," Olson said. "But even then I thought, 'OK, this is season-ending,' not realizing how truly serious it was."

Turner was rushed to the hospital, where his initial feeling proved hauntingly true. The senior had severely damaged his right leg, hyper-extending his knee and suffering ligament and nerve damage. He also faced circulation problems in his knee.

Olson recalls a surgeon announcing to everyone, "With a lot of prayers, we might be able to save his lower leg."

The leg didn't have to be amputated, but Turner has had to undergo countless hours of surgery and as many hours of rehabilitation.

Turner had one of the greatest careers in Purdue track and field history. He won four Big Ten titles and earned All-America honors twice. In one of his final jumps as a Boilermaker, he placed third at the 1999 NCAA indoor championships with a school-record effort of 53-7.5

In addition to the hundreds of cards and letters Turner received, Purdue professors sent dinner to Turner and his parents on several occasions during his hospital stay, and students offered apartment and car keys to his parents, who came to be by their son's side from Inglewood, California.

Olympic gold medalist triple jumper Mike Conley paid Turner a visit, as did 1996 gold medal winner Greg Bell. Turner received cards from such Olympic standouts as Gail Devers and Jackie Joyner-Kersee.

On May 7, 2000, just 13 months after his accident, Turner did what most thought would be impossible. After all the exhaustive rehabilitation and eight surgeries, he returned to the track one final time. Turner ran the 400-meter dash in the Captains' 400, an exhibition race at Purdue's Rankin Track and Field against captains from several other Purdue sports. He raced against Drew Brees and Adrian Beasley of the football team and Dan Swan and Evan Hayes of the men's tennis team, as well as cheerleading captain Brad Stark and close friend Neal Sinclair.

In the noncompetitive race, set up solely for Turner to have one final moment of athletic glory, the Los Angeles native came in last, but was able to finish the race, which was satisfying enough for everyone in attendance.

CHAPTER 7

2000s

Emotional Farewell

Assistant coach Bruce Weber once said Brian Cardinal "epitomized Coach [Gene] Keady's ultimate player."

So after Cardinal and the Boilermakers fell one victory short of delivering Keady to his first Final Four appearance ever at Purdue in 2000, Cardinal had difficulty keeping his composure.

The six-foot-eight, 247-pound Cardinal tried to fight back the tears, but finally couldn't hold back his emotions during the press conference after Purdue's loss to Wisconsin.

Cardinal was unable to answer the media's first question. He wept and buried his head.

After a prolonged silence, Keady interrupted and said to the media, "Try to have some compassion."

Cardinal was eventually able to answer reporters' questions about 30 minutes after the press conference in the team's locker room.

Between each sentence he took deep breaths, but broke down again when he was asked about getting so close to earning Keady that elusive Final Four trip.

"If anybody deserves it, he does," Cardinal said. "It's just too bad."

Keady pointed out how valuable Cardinal was to his team's magical run in the 2000 NCAA Tournament.

"He's the guy we leaned on to give us the emotional lifts we needed, the one to get a big shot to go down," Keady said. "He deserves better. He deserves to go to the Final Four, but we didn't get it, and he'll face it like a man and be better because of it."

When Cardinal made his final public appearance as a Boilermaker at the team's annual basketball banquet in the Purdue Memorial Union on April 19, 2000, many of the 500 or so people in attendance had tears in their eyes.

Why? Because Cardinal went out of his way to tell Keady how much he meant to him during his collegiate career.

After Cardinal had recognized everyone from his teammates to coaches to cheerleaders to fans, he turned his attention to Keady.

"I promised myself I wouldn't cry," said Cardinal, knowing that the promise wouldn't be kept.

"I would like to thank Coach Keady. He's a wonderful man. I want to thank him especially for giving me a chance to earn a degree from a Big Ten university. I appreciate him giving me a chance to be a winner, a leader ... [then the tears began flowing]. Coach, you've definitely earned my undying respect and admiration. I hope you're as proud of me as I am of you. I remember being in Coach [Jay] Price's office one time and I asked Coach Keady if years down the road if I was fortunate enough to have kids that I was hoping I could bring them back to meet him. The reason being is I'd like for my kids to meet the man who made me the person I am today. He's done a tremendous amount for me.

"Even though we didn't give him that missing piece of the puzzle by going to the Final Four, he's got a piece I don't know if he knows he has: he has a piece of my heart and I love him very much."

Keady's Tips for Looking Your Best

B oilermaker fans nationwide loved Coach Gene Keady's appearance on the *Late Show with David Letterman* on April 26, 2000.

Prior to going to commercial break, Letterman previewed Keady's appearance by saying, "When we come back we'll have the Top 10 Purdue basketball coach Gene Keady tips for good looking."

Before Keady's introduction, the show's Campaign 2000 skit, which poked fun at Keady's much-maligned hairstyle, ran. It showed Keady with one of his usual sideline scowls, and then the camera showed the top of his head. The tag line was "Purdue basketball, it will comb you over."

The show had been running the bit throughout much of April. One of the show's spokespersons said the idea for the Keady comb-over joke came from Letterman himself while the Indianapolis native was caught up in March Madness.

On one show, Letterman expressed his desire to see Keady's Boilermakers advance to the Final Four.

Letterman introduced Keady by saying, "All the way from West Lafayette, your National Association of Basketball Coaches and Big Ten Basketball Coach of the Year, Purdue University coach Gene Keady."

The "Top 10 Gene Keady Tips For Looking Your Best" were:

10. Shake head violently. If a single strand moves–keep spraying.

9. You can find some snazzy ties in the stadium lost-and-found.

8. Always comb with the grain, not against it.

7. Yelling at your players makes your face purple—that's sort of like having a tan.

6. Tight pants highlight the fact that you're a member of the "Big Ten."

5. Don't be one of those guys with hair plugs—I mean, who

do they think they're fooling?

4. I live by one simple rule: Try to look better than Dick Vitale.

3. On special occasions, I like to use a little eyeliner.

2. Never, under any circumstances, go to Letterman's barber.

1. Forget "six-pack" abs … just go for the six-pack.

After Keady read "Top 10" list, Letterman went over and shook Keady's hand and said, "I was pulling for you … during the tournament. Thanks very much."

Just before his departure to New York City, Keady said, "I'm looking forward to going to New York and promoting Purdue. This is a great opportunity to get some national exposure for Purdue and have some fun with a former Hoosier. I've always enjoyed watching Dave's show. It's very entertaining, and I've gotten a lot of laughs from it."

Dorsch Gets a Mulligan

Fate smiled on kicker Travis Dorsch, as he benefited from the greatest do-over in recent Purdue football memory.

With four seconds remaining in the 2000 game against sixth-ranked Michigan, Dorsch's 33-yard field goal snuck inside the left upright, giving Purdue a thrilling 32-31 win. It is believed to be the only time the Boilermakers have ever won a game on a field goal as time expired.

After several miscues late in the previous season, Dorsch had become the goat for many unsympathetic fans in the 10 months leading up to the game.

Dorsch was thinking he would have to endure even more intense criticism after he missed a 32-yard field goal with 2:11 left on the clock against the Wolverines. Little did he know, he would get a mulligan—a golf term for getting a second chance without penalty to hit a shot.

Dorsch said he tried to clear his mind after the first miss, but with screaming fans and frustrated teammates, it wasn't easy.

"I didn't even warm up for that second kick," Dorsch admitted. "By not warming up, I thought I would slow my leg kick down. I did just enough. When I hit it I thought it was good, but it was very close."

The Catch Heard 'Round The Boilermaker World

Nobody wanted Seth Morales to transfer to Purdue from Butler University—except Morales himself. By the evening of October 28, 2000, everyone was glad he did.

On that date at Ross-Ade Stadium, the 16th-ranked Boilermakers trailed No. 12 Ohio State 27-24 with just over two minutes remaining, their Big Ten championship hopes and Rose Bowl dreams essentially hanging in the balance. When Purdue lined up on second and 10 from its own 36-yard line, Morales was the fourth option for quarterback Drew Brees's call of 74X-Z Pole. But the crafty Morales, all five foot 10 and 171 pounds of him, was able to get behind Ohio State All-American strong safety Michael Doss, and Brees found him wide open for a game-winning 64-yard touchdown pass.

Morales, who posted season bests of seven catches and 115 yards in the game, was a walk-on for the Boilermakers in 1999 and played on the scout team after transferring from Butler. He earned a scholarship at the conclusion of 2000 training camp and went on to rank fourth on the team with 35 catches for 556 yards to go with two touchdowns.

Although the dramatic victory didn't clinch the conference title or Rose Bowl berth for Purdue, it proved to be a must-win game.

Katie Bar the Door

Katie Douglas always seemed to have a knack for coming up big when her team needed it most. The two-time All-American guard/forward made no fewer than five game-winning shots in her career.

It started as a freshman when she hit a layup with 8.8 seconds left and added a free throw with one second remaining in a 71-68 victory over Illinois on February 22, 1998. Less than a month later in the semifinals of the Big Ten Tournament on March 1, Douglas beat Iowa 61-60 with a layup with 6.5 seconds to go.

As a sophomore, Douglas sent the Boilermakers' game February 12, 1999, at Penn State into overtime with a jumper, and then she won it 76-74 with a layup with 8.6 seconds left.

In the first game of her junior season, Douglas beat home-standing Dayton 60-58 at the buzzer on November 19, 1999.

Finally, as a senior, Douglas clinched Purdue's 74-71 double-overtime victory on February 11, 2001, at Ohio State with 18 seconds remaining.

Douglas is one of only three two-time All-Americans in Big Ten history (along with Ohio State's Tracey Hall and Katie Smith), and she is the lone player in Purdue history to rank in the top 10 in career points, rebounds, assists, blocked shots and steals.

Heisman Hopefuls

Although the Boilermakers never have had a Heisman Trophy winner, they have had some worthy candidates. Among them, quarterback Bob Griese was runner-up to Florida quarterback Steve Spurrier in 1966, running back-cornerback Leroy Keyes finished second to USC tailback O.J. Simpson in 1968, and quarterback Mike Phipps was edged by Oklahoma fullback Steve Owens in 1969 in the closest vote in Heisman history.

Quarterback Drew Brees was a two-time finalist—as a junior in 1999, when he finished fourth, and a year later, when he placed third. He became the first Purdue player to wind up in the top 10 since quarterback Jim Everett in 1985.

Brees's candidacy was different from all the others. Besides having more games televised and there being more media attention on college football, technology made promoting athletes easier and, seemingly, never ending. Consider that the sports information department sent out a CD-ROM to every member of the Football Writers Association of America prior to his senior season. Then, throughout the year, it published *Drew Brees Weekly*, a comprehensive four-page update that was e-mailed to interested parties and posted on the athletics department web site for all to view. The goal was to get as much information in front of as many people as possible in hopes of increasing Brees's popularity.

Although Brees did not capture the Heisman, he did receive the Maxwell Award in 2000, presented annually to the nation's outstanding player.

Sigma Chi QBs

Bob DeMoss, Bob Griese, Mark Herrmann, Jim Everett and Drew Brees have more in common than being legendary quarterbacks for Purdue.

All five were members of Sigma Chi fraternity, as well.

When Brees was announced as winner of the Maxwell Award as the nation's outstanding player at the *ESPN Awards Show* in December of 2000, athletic public relations director Jim Vruggink congratulated him with the Sigma Chi handshake. Vruggink also is a member of the fraternity.

Dooley's No-Hitters

Johnny Vander Meer of the Cincinnati Reds threw no-hitters in consecutive starts during the 1939 season. Junior Megan Dooley of the Purdue softball team was nearly as impressive in 2000, authoring two "no-nos" in four starts over a seven-day span.

For starters, Dooley recorded the first seven-inning no-hitter in school history when she and the Boilermakers beat Temple 1-0 on February 19 in Raleigh, North Carolina. The only run came on a homer by Jesse Jones in the top of the second inning. In fact, Jones's shot was the only hit allowed by Temple pitcher Bari Lynn Pflueger. Dooley walked two and struck out two, while allowing just one ball to be hit to the outfield and inducing 16 groundball outs.

Seven days later, Dooley no-hit Iowa State in Santa Barbara, California, as the Boilermakers won 3-0 in five innings. Dooley walked one and struck out three, and did not allow a ball hit to the outfield. Outfielder Chrissy Davie socked a solo home run to pace Purdue's six-hit attack.

Pipeline to the WNBA

During the 2001 WNBA season, three of the league's 16 head coaches were former Purdue head coaches: Lin Dunn of the Seattle Storm, Nell Fortner of the Indiana Fever and Carolyn Peck of the Orlando Miracle.

A Day that Will Live in Infamy

Like all of us, Coach Joe Tiller will never forget the morning of September 11, 2001.

The Boilermaker boss was arriving on the third floor of the Mollenkopf Athletic Center when secretary Sara Watkins informed Tiller of the horrific event.

Athletics director Morgan Burke was exiting a meeting when he learned of what had happened. Once he got back to his office in the Intercollegiate Athletic Facility, he began learning more via the internet.

Linebacker Niko Koutouvides was in the middle of a building construction technology lab in Knoy Hall when a student came into the class and said a plane had crashed into the World Trade Center. He hurried home, as he was one of the thousands who immediately became concerned about the well-being of a loved one. His brother, Ari, worked across the street at the American Express Building. After the second plane hit the other tower shortly after 9 a.m., Koutouvides panicked. Eventually his mother called to tell him his brother was safe.

"Initially you didn't understand how serious it was until you saw the pictures," Burke said. "Then it was clear that it was something I had never experienced in my lifetime."

"There have been two catastrophic events since I've been around college football," Tiller said. "The first when I was a player was the assassination of JFK [in 1963], which I'll never forget. The second is September 11. In both cases, the college football world came to a stop."

That it did.

About the last thing on anyone's mind was sports, yet Purdue was scheduled to host Notre Dame four days later.

Originally Purdue officials, including Tiller, were in favor of playing the game, but in the end the game was rescheduled for December 1. The Big East, of which Notre Dame is a member in all sports except football, was one of three conferences to first announce intentions to postpone all games, joining the Pac-10 and ACC. Meanwhile, the SEC, Big 12 and Big Ten initially agreed to move forward with their schedules, though certain member schools had already called off their games.

The debate was made moot on September 13, when the NCAA announced that all games would be postponed.

It was that period of indecisiveness that was tough for Tiller. He explained that watching film on the Fighting Irish was virtually impossible.

"I couldn't watch tape," Tiller admitted. "I was sitting in my office at night when I should be watching tape and I was watching interviews with people [involved in the tragedy]. I was mesmerized by all that was happening. If the game would have been played September 15, I certainly would not have been into it."

As Fate Would Have It

Purdue might have caught a break while it was recruiting forward Chris Booker out of Tyler (Texas) Junior College.

The six-foot-10, 247-pounder had narrowed his list of schools to Purdue, Louisville and Texas Tech.

Cardinals coach Rick Pitino was scheduled to travel to the Lone Star State to see Booker, who was regarded as one of the nation's top junior college power forwards, but he never made it.

Just prior to departing for Texas, Pitino learned that tragedy struck at the World Trade Center on September 11, 2001.

Pitino's brother-in-law, William Minardi, was one of those killed in the terrorists attacks on the World Trade Center in New York City.

"On September 11, Coach Pitino was on his way to Tyler to come in and have a conference with me, but he called to apologize since he couldn't make it," Booker recalled. "He was on the runway in Louisville to come to Tyler.

"I knew his brother-in-law passed away, so I definitely understood. I thought that was pretty nice of him to take the time out and call me, considering what happened to his brother-in-law. I told him that I was sorry that his brother-in-law had been a part of the terrorist attacks.

"I knew he would be going through some family issues, and I took that as a sign that maybe Purdue was the right place for me because Purdue was my No. 1 choice the whole time."

"You Never Give Up"

Trailing 28-25 with 19 seconds remaining in regulation, the ball at its own three-yard line and no timeouts, the football team appeared headed for defeat September 29, 2001, at Minnesota. But as ESPN football guru Lee Corso would say, "Not so fast."

First, quarterback Brandon Hance found John Standeford for a 27-yard gain, then hooked up with Taylor Stubblefield for 39 yards. With the ball at the Golden Gophers' 31-yard line and one tick left on the clock, Purdue sent out its field goal unit, hoping to get off a kick before time expired. John Shelbourne calmly snapped the ball, Ben Smith held it and Travis Dorsch booted a then-career-long 48-yard field goal to send the game into overtime. It happened so fast that the two officials who normally stand beneath the goal posts could not get in position in time. But the kick was right down the middle, preventing any major controversy.

In overtime, the Boilermakers scored on their first possession, a 19-yard pass from Hance to Standeford on third and four. Minnesota's attempt to send the game into a second overtime was thwarted by Stuart Schweigert, who picked off an interception in the end zone on third and 10 from the Purdue 25-yard line, preserving a 35-28 win.

As Purdue radio color commentator Pete Quinn said on the broadcast, "You never give up." Truer words have never been spoken.

He Loves Me,
He Loves Me Not

Tim Stratton enjoyed a record-setting career as a tight end from 1998 to 2001. He shattered the school standard with 204 receptions, a figure that ranked as the third most by any player in Big Ten history at the time. As a junior, Stratton received the inaugural John Mackey Award as the nation's best tight end. He became only the fourth player in Purdue annals to be named first-team All-Big Ten on three occasions.

But Stratton had a strained relationship with head coach Joe Tiller. Stratton was a free-spirited sort who loved to have a good time on and off the field. He made a pregame ritual out of playing catch with fans in the stands, always spoke whatever was on his mind and once chest-bumped Tiller in a move that was right out of the World Wrestling Federation.

"We have a love-hate relationship," Stratton liked to say of his coach. "He loves to hate me."

Holy Toledo

Purdue's two winningest football coaches—Jack Mollenkopf and Joe Tiller—both have ties to Toledo, Ohio.

Mollenkopf, No. 1 with 84 victories, was head coach at Waite High School in Toledo from 1935 to 1946 before joining Stu Holcomb's staff at Purdue. Mollenkopf's prep teams won six city championships and three times were recognized as state champions.

Tiller, with 48 wins through the 2002 season, is a native of Toledo and graduated from Rogers High School in 1960.

Wing and a Prayer

One of the most heroic finishes in Boilermaker football history occurred November 17, 2002, at Michigan State.

Purdue, which had a 4-6 record, saw a fourth-quarter lead slip away as the Spartans scored with 7:43 remaining to claim a 42-37 lead.

With the Boilermakers' postseason chances hanging in the balance, quarterback Kyle Orton came to the rescue.

Purdue was faced with a fourth-and-eight situation from the Michigan State 40 and 3:25 left in the game. To make matters worse, starting quarterback Brandon Kirsch was hurt on third down when he was hit hard in the chest by linebacker Mike Labinjo.

Orton, who had stood on the sideline for nearly three and a half hours with the temperature barely above 30 degrees, was inserted after three or four warmup tosses.

Orton said he was freezing as he trotted onto the field.

"Everything was cold," he said. "I had trouble calling the play in the huddle because my mouth felt like it was frozen shut. I was about as cold as you could get."

Orton shook off the elements, stepped to the line of scrimmage, recognized the Spartans' man-to-man coverage and changed the play that was called. After the snap barely beat the play clock, Orton threw a perfect pass towards the end zone, hitting receiver John Standeford in stride down the left sideline for a 40-yard touchdown.

Offensive coordinator Jim Chaney said he called for a pivot play that was designed to go to receiver Taylor Stubblefield. But when Orton audibled, he brought Stubblefield in to block Michigan State's blitzing defensive back, which was exactly the right call.

"Kyle saw the matchup that he could exploit in max protection and threw a perfect pass," Chaney said. "It was remarkable what he did. I've never seen anything like that done before in my tenure in this profession."

Coach Joe Tiller later said the play was the defining moment of the 2002 season. Without question it was. It allowed the Boilermakers to appear in their sixth consecutive bowl game, a school record.

Mackey Massacre

P urdue took out a couple years of frustration out on arch-rival Indiana on January 25, 2003, in Mackey Arena.

The Boilermakers dominated the 14th-ranked Hoosiers en route to a 69-47 victory, snapping a five-game losing streak to the Cream and Crimson.

It was Purdue's first win over Indiana in 1,098 days, Coach Gene Keady's largest margin of victory over a ranked team ever and the biggest margin over Indiana by any Purdue team since the 1968-69 season.

A lot was said and written about the behavior of The Gene Pool, the name of Purdue's student section. At times, their cheers were harsh. Throughout the game, IU guard Tom Coverdale heard "Al-co-hol-ic" when he stepped to the free throw line. The cheer even drew a wicked glare from Hoosier coach Mike Davis, who suffered his worst defeat in three years as IU's coach. After he starred at the crowd for a few seconds, Davis smiled.

One fan held up a sign that poked fun at Coverdale's blood alcohol content. "Coverdale: PPG: 12.3, RPG: 3.8, BAC: .238." Coverdale had problems with alcohol consumption during high school and college.

The win by Keady's Boilermakers, who were 21-20 against Indiana's Bob Knight, was difficult for one former Knight player to stomach.

Todd Leary, a former guard for Knight who was doing color commentary for the Indiana Radio Network, had a few choice things to say about what transpired.

Following is a brief transcript of the on-air conversation between Leary and play-by-play announcer Don Fischer:

Fischer: "Well, Gene Keady just left his interview [with *ESPN-Plus* color analyst Greg Kelser] and then walked over to his wife, Pat, and gave her a kiss [laughter]."

Leary: "God bless him."

Fischer: "Everybody is feeling good today [laughter]."

Leary: "God bless him."

Fischer: "Well at any rate …"

Leary: "It takes a real man to do that [laughter]."

Fischer: "Now you're just way too bitter …"

Leary: "I tell you what, I'm not a professional, you are the utmost professional, because I don't know how you sit here and listen to this malarkey going on in this arena."

Leary later admitted his remarks were out of line and wrote a letter of apology to Keady. He also said he was sorry over the air during IU's next broadcast three days later at Michigan State.